Board of Public Charities; Pennsylvania

A Plea for the Insane in the Prisons and Poor-Houses of Pennsylvania

Board of Public Charities; Pennsylvania

A Plea for the Insane in the Prisons and Poor-Houses of Pennsylvania

ISBN/EAN: 9783744760966

Printed in Europe, USA, Canada, Australia, Japan

Cover: Foto ©ninafisch / pixelio.de

More available books at **www.hansebooks.com**

A PLEA

FOR THE

INSANE

IN THE

PRISONS AND POOR-HOUSES

OF

PENNSYLVANIA.

PHILADELPHIA:
A. C. BRYSON & CO., STEAM-POWER PRINTERS, 607 CHESTNUT STREET.
1873.

BOARD OF PUBLIC CHARITIES

OF

PENNSYLVANIA.

OFFICERS.

PRESIDENT:

GEORGE L. HARRISON,
PHILADELPHIA.

GENERAL AGENT AND SECRETARY:

DILLER LUTHER, M. D.,
READING.

MEMBERS OF THE BOARD:

GEO. L. HARRISON.	WM. BAKEWELL.
G. DAWSON COLEMAN.	A. C. NOYES.
HIESTER CLYMER.	GEORGE BULLOCK.
FRANCIS WELLS.	

STATISTICIAN:

A. J. OURT.

THE INSANE.

INSANITY, in its relation to legislation and jurisprudence, as well as to mental, moral and medical science, to its characteristics and the mode of determining its presence, as well as the method of treatment for its cure, to the best means of protecting society against its violent or mischievous assaults, as well as to its claims upon our human regard and sympathy;—is a subject of great difficulty, but, at the same time, of commensurate interest and importance.

It is not easy to give a clear

DEFINITION OF INSANITY,

and when we attempt it, the danger is that we run into one extreme or another, and either allow none to be insane but the raving maniac, or make all insane who commit anything foolish or wrong. But we need not attempt a definition here.

Whenever the condition of the raving maniac is so far approximated, and the reason sofar disordered or dethroned, that the apprehension of the distinction between right and wrong is lost, either wholly and in all relations, or partially and in relation to some particular subjects, then insanity so far exists as to demand to be specifically recognized in the administration of justice, in the means to be provided for the protection of society, and in determining the treatment due to those who are its subjects.

The diagnosis of such cases we may leave to experts, and the determination of the facts to the proper officials, judges or juries. We have nothing here to do with the question of insanity as it is presented to the psychologist or to a petit jury or to a commission *de lunatico inquirendo*, or to a board of medical examiners. In the cases to which we propose to call attention, we assume the fact of insanity to be established, and then, looking at the insane man afterwards,

WE INQUIRE WHAT IS TO BE DONE?

But we must protest, at the outset, against a certain form of mistaken feeling, which, we suspect, may very generally exist:—we refer to the disposition to regard all persons, who, being charged with crime, are acquitted on the ground of insanity, as at least highly suspicious characters, to be classed with criminals without reserve, because it happens that the greatest criminals so often seek to evade the punishment due to their crimes by setting up

THE PLEA OF INSANITY.

But this sweeping generalization is no more reasonable—especially in the case of the poor, who have no powerful friends to work for them, and cannot pay liberal fees for an elaborate defence, than it would be to regard all men as criminals and suspicious characters, who are charged with any crime, however clearly their innocence may be demonstrated; for this plea of insanity is, by no means, the only plea which is abused for the protection of knavery and violence.

As to the specious modern plea of

MORAL INSANITY,

either it must be absolutely rejected, or all administration of penal jurisprudence must, consistently, be abandoned. Any insanity, that can be recognized in law, must include a derangement or loss of the *rational* faculties, and by such derangement or loss it must be measured. A "moral insanity" which consists merely in an abnormal violence of vicious propensities, or of some particular vicious propensity, while yet the light of reason remains unabridged, and the conscious moral judgment is clear and distinct, is only another expression either for diabolical wickedness, or for the ordinary condition of human temptation.

But, waiving all such discussions, the subject which we desire to present to the practical consideration of the Legislature is this:

WHAT PUBLIC PROVISION SHOULD BE MADE FOR THE CARE AND TREATMENT OF THE INSANE, ESPECIALLY OF THE INSANE POOR,

including those who have been convicted of crime or charged with its commission.

In order to a clear exposition and apprehension of the subject which we thus desire to present, it will be advisable and even necessary to analyze it, and to distribute the insane into their several classes, with reference to the end we have in view;—to the public provision to be made for their safekeeping, care and treatment. With this view, the insane may be distributed into

THREE DIFFERENT CLASSES.

1. Those who have done no violence or public harm—the ordinary insane. These, again, fall into two sub-classes: 1. The harmless, or those from whom no harm is feared. 2. The harmful—those with manifestly dangerous and destructive propensities.

2. Those who have done harm—have committed crime—while sane, but (1) have become insane before trial or conviction; or (2) have become insane after conviction;—"insane convicts" in the strict legal sense.

3. Those who having done harm, having committed acts of violence or mischief, have been acquitted of crime on the ground of insanity.

And first, of the

INSANE WHO HAVE DONE NO HARM.

Among these, the insanity may vary in character and degree from some simple special hallucination down to complete dementia. It may include both sexes and all ages; may pro ceed from a variety of causes, moral and physical, may be recent or may have become chronic, may be more or less violent or dangerous, may be curable in various degrees, or may be absolutely incurable. These varieties may call for various medical classifications and modifications of treatment; all which we leave to medical men to arrange and determine. The classification which more directly concerns us, viewing the subject in its relation to the demand for legislative interposition or State aid, is

1. Those who have the means of support, and
2. Those who are dependent and destitute.

The first class can be cared for, either at home by their friends, or at private asylums established for the purpose. The only occasion for legislative interposition in their behalf is, to see that they have proper guardianship to secure them in the possession and right use of their property. And the only occasion for such interposition for the protection of the community in this regard, is, on the one hand, to see that friends, who undertake their guardianship, do not neglect it to the peril of the community, or abuse it to the detriment of the sufferer; and, on the other hand, to provide lest by the criminal collusion or interested misjudgment of relations and physicians, any sane person should, under certain circumstances of helplessness or exposure, be condemned to the living death of incarceration, in some private hospital for the insane :—a fate next in horror to that of being buried alive. As to what legislation is required in relation to this class, we have only to refer to the suggestions presented in our last report.

But however important the claims of this class may be upon the public consideration, they are as nothing in comparison with those of the other class of the harmless insane, viz:

THE DESTITUTE AND DEPENDENT.

To these and their sad fate, we beg once more respectfully but most earnestly, to urge the serious and special attention of the Legislature. In our former reports, we have not overlooked the claims of these helpless victims of the sorest of human maladies; but, in the discharge of our official duty, we have, repeatedly, though hitherto, perhaps, without sufficient fullness and emphasis, presented those claims to the consideration of the Legislature, and we now beg to refer to our

FORMER STATEMENTS AND SUGGESTIONS ON THIS SUBJECT.

In our report for 1870 : "More especially do we wish to denounce the cruel wrongs which the insane suffer who are inmates of almshouses. These institutions are generally wholly unsuitable for their care or even detention; or, if suitable, are presided over by persons who are entirely ignorant of the needs of this class of the sick and infirm, and whose administration is based on the crudest ideas of mental disease; it is limited to the discovery of the most available methods of preventing them from harming anything or any person but themselves. We could instance the most glaring abuses, not, as we believe, intentionally inflicted, but the result of incapacity and ignorance. The time has gone by when a disturbed imagination or a disordered intellect should be held to have converted its human victim into a distempered brute, whose home should be akin to the sty or the stable, and whose lightest restraint should be perpetual incarceration within the limits of a cell. These wrongs demand prompt redress. No hospital for the insane should remain without the constant supervision of a medical superintendent. The stewards of almshouses are never selected from any consideration of the needs of the insane."

The report was also accompanied with the following formal resolutions of the Board.

Resolved, "That the Board of Public Charities, having witnessed the evils which result from the connection of insane asylums with almshouses, and believing that a wrong is done to the insane by classing them with paupers, hindering the public from estimating aright their claims to sympathy and remedial treatment, disapprove of such an alliance, and believe that the best interests of this afflicted class of the people, and the duty of the State, concur in the establishment by the State, within a reasonable time, of sufficient accommodations for the maintenance and treatment of all the insane who may not be cared for in private hospitals."

Resolved, "That, in the judgment of the Board, all superintendents of hospitals for the insane should be members of the medical profession."

In 1871, the following, from our General Agent, was laid before the Legislature :—

"In some of our prisons, cases of insanity are found which ought to be transferred to hospitals established for the maintenance and treatment of this class of persons. In the course of my inspection of these institutions, as will be seen by a reference to my report, instances of this character have been noticed. It occasionally happens that insane persons have to be, at least temporarily, committed to a prison; but few cases can arise where this necessity exists for any great length of time. If they have been arrested for a crime, the law has made ample provision for a proper disposition of them, without a protracted confinement in a county jail, and the sooner they are removed therefrom the better, whether their incarceration is the result of crime or merely for the purpose of safe-keeping. All the better feelings of humanity, as well as a sound philanthrophy, concur in this sentiment.

"Among the various defects in our poorhouses, none are more to be deplored than that which relates to the provision made for the insane. Scarcely one can be mentioned which is not deficient in this particular. The sexes, like the arrangements in the other departments, are frequently allowed to mingle together; few have suitable accommodations for their comfort, and even in the best of them, there is a lack of sufficient attendance. New buildings have been erected in several counties, with a view to increased facilities for the support of this class, but even here, in some cases, persons have been selected who have no experience and but little qualification for the duties to which they have been assigned.

"The attention which I have given to this grave subject induces me to believe that all cases of an acute character should be placed in one of the public institutions which have been established in the State, City, or County, with a view to their treatment. To place a recent case where no suitable medical treatment or other proper attendance can be had, is either simply to leave it to nature or facilitate its passage into a chronic condition. To render an institution suitable for the successful management of such cases, nearly all the means essential for such a purpose are wanting. A proper construction of the building, where a favorable classification of the inmates can be maintained, where all the modern improvements for in-door comforts and amusements and outdoor exercise and recreation, and where competent medical and other attendance can always be procured, are necessary to attain the great object in view—a restoration to health and a sound mind.

"For the most part all that can be expected in our county almshouses is to secure such provision for the chronic and incurable insane, as will meet the demands of a Christian humanity. To confine them in close and badly ventilated apartments, with scarcely any of the comforts which an enlightened philanthropy would suggest—a condition in which they are too often found,—manifests such a failure of duty as to bring odium and shame upon the civilization of the age.

"In New York, a State institution was established in 1865 under the name of the Willard Asylum for the Insane, for the reception, care and treatment of the chronic insane poor, who were then provided for in the several county poorhouses in the State. This institution is reported to be in successful operation. Whether the plan of separating this class of insane from the more acute and hopeful cases, and keeping them in different institutions is best adapted to the successful treatment of the insane population, is a question much discussed among experts of the present day. The medical superintendents of our insane hospitals, after a full and able discussion of the subject, came to the conclusion, that such a classification would be detrimental to the interests of both classes. With such able authority against such a measure, I am not prepared to endorse the action of the New York Legislature, but prefer to leave the subject for further experience, and the candid consideration of philanthropists."

In 1872, the Board says in its report: "What the condition of the insane is, as a general rule, in the poorhouses of the State, we set forth clearly in our earliest report, and although there has been since then a manifest improvement in their condition and treatment, in several of the county establishments, it is impossible, from the circumstances which characterize the whole arrangement, discipline, and government of such institutions, that these invalids can be otherwise than grossly neglected and foully wronged; for, *at the best*, they are merely confined in places of detention, under the guardianship of a respectable overseer, who is wholly ignorant of their disease, and of the means necessary for its alleviation or its cure. We say, *at the best*. We hesitate to describe the reverse of the picture. It would exibit a scene of as cheerless and uncomforted misery as the most bitter misanthrope could desire to look upon. It is hardly fair to claim that we have passed beyond the ignorance and barbarity of the middle ages, in our consideration and care of this class of unfortunates, so long as we suffer the glaring abuses which are prevalent in our midst to continue unredressed.

"It is inconceivable to every reflecting mind, that abuses can be heaped upon the defenceless victims of this saddest of disorders, who should rather be the objects of the most spontaneous sympathy and the most willing kindness and consideration. The reasons that the chances of exposure are too remote to be estimated, and, as in the case of the child and the brute, that resistance is impossible, no doubt give impunity to the foul wrong-doing which the insane frequently suffer. But the most fruitful cause of this evil is the incompetency of those who are set over them. It is an evil almost irremediable, under the present system of appointments in the county almshouses and county jails. It generally happens that these are based solely upon political considerations. Some useful partizan must be rewarded or in some way helped, and he is given an office, the duties of which he feels in no wise called upon to discharge; having earned its perquisites by political services before he received it; and, feeling his position secure, is quite naturally led to neglect his trust, by ignoring its most essential requirements. Unfitness of the highest measure is the character of such appointments generally; and the victims in this case are a class of defenceless invalids, whose circumstances appeal with especial deserving to the highest claims of humanity and justice.

"This mode of appointment should be abolished, rather than extended, and we earnestly invoke the action of your honorable bodies to revoke all legislation which favors it. The institutions established by the State and the counties, at so great a cost, and supported from year to year by large expenditure of the public funds, extracted often by onerous taxation, should be managed after a principle which will secure those objects to accomplish which they were respectively founded."

As to the statistics in regard to this class of unfortunates, this Board hereby renews the offer made last year: "We are prepared, upon a call of either branch of the Legislature, to report upon the whole subject, stating the numbers and condition of this class, how they are now circumstanced, what proportion are probably chronic, and what curable cases, what additional accommodations are needed, and, if required, a scheme for realizing the demand which is made upon the State for the complete fulfilment of this imperative duty."

But as to the number of these helpless sufferers, these dependent wards of the State, we may say beforehand, and without reference to statistics, that, if the number is some thousands, their moral claim upon the State, as a matter of simple duty on her part, is multiplied so many thousand fold; and if the number is small, there is the less excuse for shrinking from the performance of that duty—for making proper and complete provision for the care and treatment of them all.

If these persons are to be allowed to live among us; if they are not to be left, some to starve and perish, and others to spread their mischief far and wide, it is for

THE INTEREST OF THE STATE

that public provision should be made for their detention and maintenance; and if they are to be detained and supported at the public expense, it is for the interest—the palpable, pecuniary interest of the State, that they should have appropriate and comfortable accommodations, kind supervision, and the most patient and skillful curative treatment. This may be demonstrated in a few words. We may take two facts as well ascertained, and we believe they are admitted without a dissenting voice, (1) that under proper care and skillful treatment—as in our best hospitals—about 75 per cent. of recent cases of insanity will be cured in the first six or twelve months; (2) in poorhouses, not more than 7 per cent. will be cured in the first year. Assuming these premises, and making the expense of each patient in the hospital twice what it would be in the almshouse, the gain in the first instance, under hospital treatment, is simply enormous. But this is not all. There are likely to be more cures afterwards under the skillful treatment than under the other. But suppose there were not, and that all the remaining cases were incurable, there would remain, on one side, 93 incurables to be maintained for life, and, on the other, 25; and if the ratio of expense were still double, the result would be in favor of hospital treatment as $50 to $93. That is to say, the latter method would be a continual saving to the State for many subsequent years of more than 46 per cent. per annum. Nor is this all. It must be remembered that the greater part of

THE INSANE POOR OWE THEIR POVERTY TO THEIR INSANITY,

and not their insanity to their poverty; and that, in losing their power to support themselves, they have lost also, in a very large proportion of cases, the power to support families more or less numerous, who thus become dependent upon the public for their maintenance. The restored maniac resumes not only the enjoyment of a man's consciousness, but of a man's activity—the power of self-support; and not only this, but of supporting by his industry those dependent upon him; and every man who, by his enterprise, skill, and labor, supports himself and his family, contributes also to the support of other men and their families. Such are the economical advantages accruing to the State from a proper treatment of the insane poor, and their consequent restoration to mental health.

But these unfortunate persons have claims upon the State higher far than mere considerations of economy. They are her wards, and she is bound by the dictates of

SIMPLE JUSTICE AND IMPERATIVE DUTY

to secure to them that humane, watchful, and patient care, and that skillful treatment, which will give the best promise of their speedy restoration. If she chose to put them out of the way, like noxious beasts, or to let them alone to starve and die, she might say that charity and philanthropy were no part of her mission, and ask who made her their keeper? But when she has laid her hand upon them, put them in places of restraint and detention, and taken control and charge of them, *she has made herself their keeper*, and has bound herself so to treat them, as shall most conduce to their future well-being, as well as to her own.

As to their actual

CONDITION IN OUR COUNTY POORHOUSES OR PRISONS,

we do not propose to weary the patience or offend the sensibilities of the honorable members of the Legislature by the renewed recital of the more than three times thrice told tale of the woes and sufferings of this sorely stricken class of our fellow-citizens. That the story, with all its touching and terrible details, ranging from the intensely sad to the unspeakably horrible, should have been so often repeated, and yet the evil remain to so large a degree unremedied, instead of exciting our impatience, should raise our shame, and provoke us to immediate and energetic action. The story can never grow old or worn, as long as the subject-matter itself remains a fresh and living reality. There is

BUT ONE VOICE IN THIS CASE.

No intelligent person has ever made a general visitation of the prisons and almhouses of this State without being startled and almost overwhelmed by the forlorn and hopeless and sometimes horrible condition of their insane inmates. Those who some years since made a similar visitation in the State of New York pronounced their condition "deplorable," and that State forthwith determined to apply an effectual remedy. The impressions made upon this Board by similar visitations in our own State have been laid before the Legislature in our reports from year to year. The shocking and sickening revelations, so graphically set forth in the memorial of Miss Dix, presented to the Legislature of 1845, are not yet obsolete. There have been some improvements since made in some of these places. In the Philadelphia Almshouse, since then, there has been a great reform; and in several other counties, well constructed hospitals for the sick and insane have been built; but, with one or two exceptions, there is no special medical supervision or paid attendance at all. But in most parts of the State that condition remains now substantially the same as then. Indeed, without

A TOTAL REVOLUTION OF THE SYSTEM

it is impossible greatly to improve it. There may be grave faults in the management of these poorhouses, some of which might be remedied, and others are probably incapable of remedy; but the great fault—the fundamental cause of the evil, is in the system itself. If the administration were made as perfect as human infirmity allows, if the best superintendents or wardens, and the most faithful attendants were secured, while the evil might be mitigated, it would remain substantially the same, until the system itself is changed. The remedy is not reform but revolution.

We take leave to insert here the report made in the course of the present year by a member of this Board, of his personal inspection of one of our county poorhouses.

"With respect to the strictly pauper department of this almshouse, it bore a resemblance to other establishments. There was a scene of listless idleness and uselessness, without any superintending care. My attention was particularly directed by the general agent to the hospital for the insane, which was a separate building, upon the same ground with the other departments of the almshouse. I found these inmates suffering for the want of almost every attention and consideration which are necessary to make life, even to the strong and hardy, tolerable. They have sufficient food, such as it is, at stated intervals, and the cells they occupy are furnished generally with a rough bed and bed-clothes. These cells, too, are *tolerably* clean, for the cleansing of an establishment such as this, can be done without much difficulty, because there is always a sufficient number of paupers to do the work. Where the insane patients are considered violent or even disagreeable, it often happens that their cells are either neglected, or forcible measures are resorted to for the purpose of overcoming their interference, while their cells are being cleaned by the paupers. Though the board had previously called the attention of the directors of this institution to the imperfect ventilation of the insane hospital, I found that even the means available for correcting the cause of this complaint, had been very imperfectly attended to. The consequence was that the atmosphere of most of the cells had become so vitiated and offensive that any person accustomed to the open air, would necessarily have fainted upon remaining within the apartment for a moment of time. The inmates seemed to have become used to this noxious atmosphere, and they did not complain of it. On the contrary, the only complaint on their part was that made by an old woman, when her window was lowered a little to admit the fresh air.

THE RESPONSIBILITY FOR THIS CHRONIC NEGLECT OF THESE CLASSES

begins with the public and ends with the humblest attendant of the institution. So lost to all sense of decency have the insane in this hospital become, by reason of the failure on the part of those in authority to encourage a proper appreciation of self-respect among the inmates, that their habits are precisely like those of a brute. Consequently many of them are kept naked in their cells, from which they are drawn out each morning to be cleaned and their rooms put in order. The filthiest part of the litter—for their bedding consists wholly of straw—is then removed and its place supplied with a similar quantity of the fresh material; when they are returned to their disgusting dens, there to pass another period of solitary wretchedness in an atmosphere whose odor exceeds in offensiveness, anything which the imagination can conceive. Through the gradual enfeebling of the higher attributes of their natures, some of these people come to be regarded by the other inmates as mere animals, and the young girls of the establishment look upon these naked men simply as they would look upon a horse or a hog. I am told that frequently two of the young female inmates of this insane hospital are called upon to clean these men each morning as they are drawn out from their cells."

The following statement of the condition of the insane in another poorhouse, is given on the well-sustained authority of another member of the Board.

"In February last a visit was paid this almshouse, and an insane inmate was seen,—a young women over twenty years of age, whose whole dress consisted of a thin chemise with short sleeves, a single skirt, and a pair of shoes. When brought before the visitors a borrowed cloak was thrown over her shoulders. She was blue with cold and utterly filthy in person. Her cell had the appearance of having undergone a recent hasty washing, but was pervaded with an odor loathsome in the extreme. On the day of this visit the thermometer fell to 14 degrees."

"In March another visit was paid to the institution by several gentlemen in a body. Only one portion of the building was visited, which is supposed to be devoted exclusively to women. In one cell was a young woman, the one already referred to. Her cell was without any furniture whatever, her bed consisted of one blanket, her clothing a ragged chemise open to her waist, and one scanty skirt and a pair of shoes. She was indescribably unclean, and alive with vermin. Her cell reeked with a sickening odor, the result of a total absence of all conveniences for cleanliness. She shivered with cold, while in the presence of her visitors; the thermometer standing, at the time, several degrees below the freezing point.

"Opposite to the cell, which we have very faintly described, was another. The short day had already faded into dusk, and as the light was thrown through the little aperture in the door, it fell upon two wretched women, both of whom were absolutely without a single garment to cover them. One of the poor creatures sat crouching in the corner with a small blanket drawn across her shoulders, while the other was crawling on all fours on the floor, without even this poor apology for any remnant of human decency! There was not a particle of furniture in the cell; and there, on this wintry March night, in an atmosphere which the witnesses declare to have been utterly horrible, were these two human beings, brought down far below the level of our domestic brutes.

"In an adjoining cell the visitors found a man lying on an old mattress, the only sign of furniture which they saw in either of the rooms inspected. They were informed that the inmate was a woman; but upon one of the gentlemen calling to him, he sat up, and it was seen that it was a man. The attendant with some confusion explained that he must have been brought in while he was away.

"We found the female insane department in a shocking condition; so bad that it would be impossible to give a description of the place on paper. In some cells there were two or more women confined; some without any clothing, lying on the floor, without mattress, carpet or any thing else, except an old government blanket. The place had a horrible putrid odor.

"We examined one woman who was quite young. I was afraid to go near her, as she seemed covered with vermin. We were all much shocked by the visit, and I think I shall remember it as long as I live."

And the General Agent reports the following amongst many similar instances of abuses and neglects in the same establishments:

"Insane totally neglected, morally, physically and medically; less attention is given to them, than would be given to the lowest animals; four are incapable of self care, confined in filthy cells; one, a female, has great neighborhood notoriety, from sad incidents connected with her history; known as an intelligent, esteemed and attractive young lady, the daughter of a well-known inhabitant of the neighborhood, she fell a victim to the arts of the seducer. Insanity is alleged to have been caused by her disappointment. This occurred twenty-one years ago. The sad case is rendered still more painful by her present forlorn condition. A bed of straw, upon a damp dirty floor, into which the external light can find no entrance, is the only furniture. A seat, a chair or a bench, has apparently never been furnished; the consequence of which is that the muscles of the lower extremities, from the cramped position in which she was always found, have become permanently contracted; so that the only movement of which she is capable, is one similar to that of a frog."

"An unusually large number of insane; many of chronic form, but quite a number of strongly marked cases, who were confined, and had been chained to the floor until released by my direction. A young girl of seventeen years of age confined in a gloomy cell; since removed by my request to the State Hospital, where she is gradually being restored."

"Twenty-two insane, twelve are kept in close confinement, some in chains; one always chained to the ceiling to prevent him from tearing his clothes; some entirely nude; at least six with straw litters; not one of the twelve was ever removed into the open air. All confined in apartments opposite each other, a narrow corridor extending between them. The effect of this close proximity was, to make the day and night hideous, with the distressing shrieks and yells of the wretched and mal-treated madmen."

"Eight insane, one of whom handcuffed, one hobbled; one female confined to her room."

"One hundred and thirty-five inmates, four blind, one palsied, seven idiots; seven cells in the basement, with insane in each, in a revolting condition."

"Twenty insane; of these about eight were confined, not to their uncomfortable cells only, but restrained by iron fetters, long after the necessity had passed away. These were removed at my instigation and the doors of their cells were opened, to give them the benefit of the open air and exercise, with decided improvement in their condition."

There are two difficulties in the way of checking

THESE AND SIMILAR ABOMINATIONS:

One is the unwillingness of the Directors of the poor to make expenditures for the comfort and well-being of the classes committed to their charge. They employ a steward whose principal requisite is that he shall be a good farmer, and whose attention must be given mainly to the farm of the institution, which may be, in extent, from 100 to 400 acres. As a consequence, the care and supervision of the human beings, over whom this "steward" is placed, are lost sight of, to a great degree, in the apparently more important business of the farm, and are generally committed to the oversight of the paupers themselves. This is one evil. The other is apparent in the very unsuitable arrangement and construction in which the most helpless inmates—we mean the insane—are placed. In these structures it is a rare thing to find the sexes at all adequately separated, and, generally, they have no airing grounds, or even yards, to which the patients can repair and refresh themselves during the day. Therefore, they must remain in seclusion within their cells, from the beginning to the end of the year, existing in an atmosphere of great impurity, and constantly deteriorating in their mental and physical condition.

In order to make the work of the Board effective, a certain amount of

EXECUTIVE POWER

should be granted to it; as has recently been conferred upon the New York Board of Public Charities, by the Legislature of that State. The public seem to be satisfied with

HOUSES OF DETENTION:

To get the various classes of unfortunates out of sight, seems to be the main object. The consequence is, that, as a general rule, the

PRISON IS BETTER THAN THE POORHOUSE,

as a receptacle for the insane.

We may lay it down as a principle, at length become too plain to be controverted; indeed as a point admitted on all hands, that poorhouses are not, and cannot be made fit places for the care and treatment of the insane. That they may receive proper treatment with any hope of recovery, they must be placed in hospitals or asylums, especially constructed and fitted up for their accommodation, with cheerful scenes within and cheerful scenery around, with skilled medical supervision and carefully selected and well trained attendants; none of which conditions can be commanded in, or in connection with an ordinary county poorhouse. In connection with so large an establishment as the Philadelphia Almshouse, where are gathered nearly one-half of all the pauper population of the State, a separate hospital of the required character may be provided and supported; and we commend the humane and earnest spirit which is engaged in two or three of the larger communities, as, for instance, Berks and Lancaster Counties—in making adequate provision for their insane. But in connection with the smaller almshouses of the several counties, and still more in connection with the township arrangements for the care of the poor, such separate hospital accommodations are out of the question. They will never be established, and, if they were, they could not be maintained.

It will naturally be asked here, whether the State has not already established one or more

GENERAL HOSPITALS FOR THE CARE OF THE INSANE,

with a view of meeting this precise difficulty? She has; and established them, professedly, for this very class of the insane, whose case we are now considering—for the insane poor, the insane who had been or are liable to be, gathered into the almshouses, or sent for safe-keeping to the prisons, in the several counties. The State has established these hospitals at no little expense;

BUT A VERY SMALL PERCENTAGE OF THE "POOR" INSANE ARE NOW IN THEM;

the great mass still remain in their former wretched, forlorn and hopeless quarters, a spectacle of misery or a butt of derision; and an element of disturbance and irritation to the rest of the inmates. To the hospital at Harrisburg there were committed by the public authorities and courts during the year 1872, sixty-one poor patients and one hundred and thirty-eight "paying" patients were sent there by "friends." And of the four hundred and eight remaining on Dec. 31, 1872, there were one hundred and seventy-nine supported by "public authorities" and two-hundred and twenty-nine by "friends of patients." Again, of the one hundred and sixteen patients committed to this hospital during the nine months ending Sept. 30, 1873, eighty-four were "paying" and only thirty-two public or indigent insane patients.

Now it is manifest from the memorial of Miss Dix, in response to which the State Hospital was established, and by the express words of the law of 1845, coeval with its establishment, that the original design of the hospital was what that of any such hospital ought, in all reason,—to be, to provide for

THE INSANE POOR.

The law, section 25, declares that, in order of admission the "poor" shall have precedence of the "rich," (defined throughout the act "paying patients") and while the finances of the State do not permit ample provision for all cases of insanity, recent cases shall have precedence over cases of long standing. If, under this law, the whole capacity of the hospital were devoted to the "poor," no objection, perhaps, could be made to sending away the incurable, after a reasonable period of trial, to make room for recent cases; although it does not appear that such was the intention of the law, which seems to have merely laid down a "rule" to govern the order of admission to vacancies as they should be found to exist. But how should it happen that a majority of the inmates of this State institution should be "paying" patients?

How happens it that during the year 1872, sixty-nine per cent. of the patients admitted were paying patients, and only thirty-one per cent. public patients, and of those admitted during the nine months ending Sept. 30, 1873, the paying patients should increase to seventy-two per cent. with a corresponding reduction of public patients to twenty-eight per cent. Again, that at the close of the year 1872 this hospital should be occupied with fifty-five per cent. of paying patients, and at the end of Sept. 30, 1873, with fifty six per cent. of the same class?

Is it said that the incurables are sent away to make room for recent cases. But upon what authority? And, besides, if those sent to the hospital by their friends are recent and curable cases, in a larger proportion than the others, how comes it that a smaller percentage of these are discharged during the year? Or, if they are incurable in a larger proportion than those committed by the public authorities, why are they not sent away in still greater proportion than the others, instead of being discharged in still less proportion? Or, rather, why are they not all sent away; or rather kept away, as long as any of the others remain unprovided for? We understand that, as a general rule, those committed to this hospital by the county authorities, if not "speedily" curable, are sent back to the helpless and hopeless life-doom of the poorhouses. On the other hand it is evident that "paying" patients may stay as long apparently as their comfort and the convenience of their friends require, and their means suffice for their support. Now we cannot but regard all this as a gross public wrong. The State has erected hospitals,

NOT FOR THE "RICH," BUT FOR THE "POOR;"

or, for the rich only when the poor should all be provided for. There is no need, even if it were right, that the State should erect hospitals at the public expense and out of the public taxes, for the accommodation of the rich; they can or they will provide hospitals for themselves, including persons of moderate means as well as of considerable wealth. We maintain that the entire capacity of the State hospitals should be appropriated to the poor patients, before any such are refused admission or sent away under any pretext whatever. The hospital at Dixmont, though a *private* charitable corporation, and only aided by the State, comes much nearer to our idea of the duty and the intention of the State in this regard, than that at Harrisburg. At the former, there remained at the close of the year 1872, only 117 private patients out of a total of 446; and on Sept. 30, 1873, only

23.89 per cent. of "paying" patients, or 108 out of a total of 452.

And, again, of the 116 patients received into the State Hospital at Harrisburg, during the nine months, ending September 30, 1873, 84 of them or nearly three-fourths were "paying" patients; while, for the same period, out of 173 patients admitted to the hospital at Dixmont, only 72 or about two fifths were "paying" patients. In other words 80.79 per cent. more *private* patients were received into the State Hospital for the "insane poor," at Harrisburg, than into the private hospital for the insane (aided by the State) at Dixmont.

It may be said, and perhaps with truth, that in many cases, the friends of insane patients, who can furnish the smaller sum required at the State Hospital for their support, would not be able to meet the heavier charges of a private asylum; and that, therefore, such insane patients must be thus admitted at the hospital or sent to the poorhouse. This idea seems highly plausible, and might at first receive favor from inconsiderate persons. But upon reflection it clearly appears unsound in theory ; and upon experience it proves highly objectionable. If these patients are *poor*, why should precisely this class of poor patients have precedence of those who are still poorer ? And if they are rich—as by the terms of the statute all "paying" patients are, then the law expressly gives the poor the precedence over them. Besides all these

MIDDLE MEASURES OF GIVING PUBLIC AID TO THE POOR,

are found in practice to be dangerous, and liable to great abuses on the part both of the recipients and the almoners of the public bounty. This case has proved itself, in our judgment, no exception to the general rule.

It may be suggested that it has been thought well to have some *paying* patients in order to give

RESPECTABILITY TO THE INSTITUTION.

We can scarcely listen to the suggestion with patience, or

answer it with calmness. If all the poor were already provided for and accommodated, the suggestion might pass; although *we* should not make it. We should never propose that the State should tax herself to furnish hospital accommodations to the rich in any case, whether by way of gratuity or of profitable speculation. But that is not the case. The poor are not all enjoying the care and treatment of the hospitals; and shall they by the hundred and the thousand continue to languish into idiocy, or rave out their miserable lives in the cells of prisons with malefactors and felons, or in the more foul and wretched and hopeless receptacles of county poorhouses, in order that the hospital, which receives a few score of them, may be respectable, and its superintendent and officers may not find themselves in charge of an institution of mere paupers?

But, finally, it may be said, as a partial explanation of the great comparative rapidity with which the poor who are committed to the hospital are sent away, that a large part of them—those committed by the courts—are

PERSONS CHARGED WITH CRIME

who have been acquitted on the ground of insanity. Under the present law this explanation must, to a certain extent, be accepted; but as these persons do not fall under the general class of the insane now under consideration, viz: those who have done no harm, and are free from any charge of crime, their case is reserved for consideration in the sequel.

In the class of harmless insane, we include, it will be remembered, all those who are legally charged with no acts of mischief, violence or crime; as well, therefore, those, from whom such acts may be apprehended, as those, who, from their apparently gentle and inoffensive habits, are the objects of no such fear. Whether there be any of the insane so entirely harmless, that they can be trusted with absolute confidence, needing no special watch or restraint, some have doubted, and we need not decide or discuss the question; for, in our clear judgment, there is no good reason why those who may need greater degrees of watchful care and restraint, should not be treated in the same establishments with those who may need less, especially as the distinction is merely one of varying degrees. Even those who exhibit the greatest developments of insane cunning for mischief, or are subject to the fiercest paroxysms of violence, or even of homicidal impulse, may be kept with proper classifications and internal arrangements, in the same institution with patients of the greatest gentleness and quietness of temper and demeanor. At all events, the proper hospital, with its more skillful superintendence and its more varied and thorough appliances, is, of all others, precisely the place for the former class; for in poorhouses they can scarcely be kept at all, except as wild beasts; and prisons are not places to which justice or humanity can doom the innocent and helpless madman, however violent or dangerous. Yet are not such poor defenceless unfortunates, if adjudged too dangerous to go at large, and pronounced not curable, habitually sent to rave and rot in the foul dens of a poorhouse, or in the dungeons of a prison, there to be classed with robbers and murderers?

The importance of having the State Hospitals for the Insane, subjected in this and in other respects, to the

SUPERVISION OF SOME PARTY NOT CONNECTED WITH THEIR IMMEDIATE MANAGEMENT,

so that the rights of the poor may be more surely, steadily, and systematically protected, we reserve for fuller consideration further on. But we cannot omit to observe here, that the State hospitals for the insane poor were not devised originally at the suggestion of *experts*; but upon the painstaking investigations and earnest petitions of Miss Dix and other benevolent persons; and it is highly reasonable that their management, particularly as regards the receiving and discharge of patients, should be placed under the visitatorial power of disinterested parties, concerned only in securing the good to be derived from them for the defenceless insane poor. It is not to be supposed, however, that, under any management, sufficient provision has yet been made in our State hospitals for

ALL THE INSANE POOR IN THE COMMONWEALTH.

Such provision ought to be made with all possible despatch. To propose to make it is no wild or visionary or extravagant scheme. It can be made in Pennsylvania as well as in New York. And we have already shown, that if we are to take care of the insane poor at all at the public expense, the most economical method, irrespective of the demands of humanity, is to gather them into well-managed hospitals, instead of leaving them to linger out a miserable existence, hopeless of restoration, in prisons and poorhouses.

We proceed now to consider the case of the two other classes of the insane.

II. Those who, while sane, have committed acts of violence or crime, but have either

1. Become insane before arraignment, and so have never been tried; or,

2. Have become insane after conviction—insane convicts.

3. Those who were insane at the time of committing such acts, and who, therefore, have been acquitted of crime on the ground of their insanity. These fall into various subdivisions to be mentioned hereafter.

These two classes (1) those who stand charged or convicted of committing acts of violence or mischief *while sane;* and (2) those, who, although charged with crime for the commission of such acts, have been acquitted on the ground of insanity at the time of their commission, we place together, not to identify or confound them under any such denomination as "criminal insane," but rather in order the more emphatically to contradistinguish them.

We begin with the case of the first of these classes; and the question is, what disposition is to be made of the insane, who stand charged with, or have been convicted of, crime.

And first of those who may, with some propriety, be called "criminal insane," *i. e.*, those who are charged with the commission of crime while sane, but who have become insane before arraignment; and who, consequently, have never been convicted or tried. Their case is a somewhat delicate one in a legal as well as a moral point of view. According to legal principles, it would seem that their detention cannot be regarded as a punishment, for they are

NOT TO BE PRESUMED GUILTY,

because they are charged with crime, nor until they are found guilty upon trial and proof; but in their present condition they are not capable of pleading, and, of course, cannot be put upon their trial. Both as accused and as dangerous persons, they may properly be kept under detention and restraint; but neither in fact nor in feeling, are they to be classed with felons or looked upon as tainted with crime, or as suffering a penalty. The fact of their present lunacy may be ascertained and established without the intervention of a jury, by the court itself, or by a commission appointed for the purpose; but their having committed the criminal acts laid to their charge, and having committed them in a sound state of mind, can be ascertained and determined only by the intervention and verdict of a jury; and any investigation or inquiry in that direction, instituted without such intervention, and without a hearing of the defendant, must necessarily be merely *ex parte*. And it is but the natural course of things, when a poor, friendless man, in his squalor and raggedness, is arraigned before a court, under the charge of some atrocious crime, accompanied with the confident allegation that, whatever may be his present mental condition, he was sane up to and at the time of the commission of the acts charged against him—it is but the natural course of things, that such a man is easily believed and presumed to be guilty; and as society must at all events, be protected from his violence, whether sane or insane, he is consigned, side by side, with the convicts and felons, to the safe keeping of a prison cell.

But surely this ought not to be so—in all reason it ought not to be so. The State owes it to her own self-respect, to her own sense of justice, if not to her sentiments of humanity, not to consign to the odium and punishment of crime, one of her citizens whose guilt has never been duly ascertained. What then shall be done with such persons? That is a serious question, and we shall endeavor to answer it. But, for the present, we only say, what is clear in the face of the matter, that they ought

NOT TO BE PLACED IN PRISON,

or in any department of a prison; and they ought to be placed where they not only will be effectually restrained from doing harm, but where they will have the best curative treatment, and the best prospect of being restored from their fearful malady.

THE CASE OF INSANE CONVICTS,

that is, of those who become insane after conviction, and while undergoing the punishment of crime, is different from the foregoing in several important particulars. For these the question of guilt is presumed to have been duly ascertained, and that they are suffering a just punishment. But in the midst of it, the mind loses its balance, and they become lunatics. Supposing this point to be ascertained and admitted—and the feigning of madness is pretty easily detected—then they are no longer responsible beings; they are no longer proper subjects of prison discipline. It is utterly unreasonable and unjust, as well as inhuman, to continue

TO INFLICT PUNISHMENT ON A MANIAC,

who neither knows the reason, nor the end, nor the idea of rightful punishment. It is as absurd as to inflict indignities or violence upon the dead body of a criminal; it is even more malignant, for the dead body has no sense of pain, but the maniac has.

Besides, the State owes it to these helpless beings, who, while under her enforced control and guardianship, have been smitten down with the most terrible of maladies—owes it to them as a mere matter of right, to give them the most skillful and promising curative treatment in her power, to save them, if possible, from confirmed and permanent mania or imbecility. To suffer a convict to become, from neglect, an incurable lunatic is worse, unspeakably worse than to dismiss him, at the expiration of his sentence, bereft of sight or hearing, or crippled by loss of limbs, or under some chronic bodily disease, in consequence of a reckless neglect of the proper medical care and treatment at the proper time. These irremediable losses and disabilities formed

NO PART OF HIS SENTENCE.

The State is bound, so far as she reasonably can, to discharge the convict, at the close of his term of punishment, in at least as good a condition—mental, moral, and physical —as that in which she received him. And, for failing in this, it will not do to seek an excuse in the small number, or the unworthy character of those who may suffer the wrong. The State, the very fountain of justice, she who takes it upon herself to punish wrongs, is bound to do no wrong to even one, and that one the meanest and most undeserving of her citizens. If there are but few convicts who need surgical or medical treatment, whether for bodily or mental diseases, so much the less excuse is there, at least on the ground of economy, for neglecting them.

Nor is this all. Even of those who are strictly insane convicts in the legal sense, and it is of those only we are now treating—*i.e.* of those who have been convicted of crime, as having been sane both at the time of the commission and the conviction, but being found insane afterwards—even of these it would be easy to show that by far the larger number were probably

INSANE BEFORE CONVICTION, AND EVEN AT THE TIME OF THE COMMISSION

of the alleged offence. It is the rich and respectable offender, who has friends and money, who can fee lawyers, who can procure and array a crowd of witnesses in his behalf, who can protract his trial, clog the wheels of justice, and make interest by his audacity—it is he who too often escapes from merited punishment under a mistaken verdict of insanity. But

THE POOR FRIENDLESS MAN,

who has been seized in some terrible act of atrocity, though committed under the impulse of actual insanity, is swiftly arraigned; and having nobody of any consideration or influence, who personally cares for him, to stand by him or advise him; without testimony, and, from his very unsoundness of mind, perhaps, neither caring or knowing how to procure it, the evidence against him ample and clear, his defence provided by the court being merely professional and perfunctory, and, of course, under such circumstances, both hasty and imperfect,

HE IS FORTHWITH CONVICTED AND SENTENCED TO THE PENITENTIARY OR THE GALLOWS.

That this is no fancy picture, but a familiar matter of fact, is established by an abundance of proof. The uniform testimony of those who have charge of jails and penitentiaries, is, that almost all the so-called insane convicts under their charge were

INSANE WHEN BROUGHT TO PRISON,

and so were almost certainly insane when tried, and probably so when they committed the offences for which they were convicted.

Dr. Compton, in charge of the State Lunatic Asylum of Mississippi, says: "My own experience with insane criminals leads me to feel rather charitable towards them. I have had only three, and there have been circumstances connected with each of these cases, which lead me to think they were insane before committing the crime."

Of the eighteen prisoners reported insane in the Eastern

Penitentiary in 1852, the Inspectors declare that "three had been placed in the penitentiary for safe keeping only, and

NOT FOR CRIME,

and had already been confined in its cells, one nearly three, one over three, and one over seven years! Eleven of the remaining fifteen were more or less insane when they were received into the penitentiary, two of the others became so a few months after, one a year, and one about four years after his reception. It will thus be seen that a large proportion were insane in a greater or less degree when first sentenced to the penitentiary; and all but one or two of the rest developed it shortly after. The observation and experience of the Inspectors have convinced them that the commission of crime is more frequently connected with mental disease than courts and juries (far less the public,) suspect:—hence the necessity of a prompt removal of all, who are found to be thus afflicted, to a place where proper treatment may restore them to mental health, and, as a consequence, to moral rectitude." Nor did this state of affairs cease at a later period. In their report for 1862, the Inspectors repeat that "There are yearly received into this Penisentiary insane convicts, insane or of diseased mental condition, on their admission." And again, in 1863: "The Inspectors again ask the Legislature to require the State Lunatic Asylum to take insane convicts, or to make an appropriation for their medical treatment in the Penitentiary. When so many convicts are known to be insane on reception into this prison, this course is wise, humane and necessary."

There are now about twenty of these "insane criminals" in the two penitentiaries, all of whom, according to the reports of the wardens, were insane or imbecile when received there. We insert here the report of Mr. Townsend, warden of the Eastern Penitentiary, made on this subject in October last: and, also, that of Capt. Wright, warden of the Western Penitentiary, made on November 24th.

REPORT OF WARDEN TOWNSEND.

"E. S. PENITENTIARY, *October* 24, 1873.

" To GEO. L. HARRISON, ESQ.,
" President of the Board of State Charities.

" Dear Sir,—I sent you a list some time ago of eleven persons confined in this penitentiary who were more or less insane. Since that time one has died, and one was pardoned by the Governor of the State, leaving now in confinement, nine. The one who was pardoned is now an inmate of an insane asylum. The nine who remain were all noted on our physician's book as '*insane*,' or '*mentally unsound*' at the time of admission. One was sent here *twenty-three years* and *ten months* ago, charged with assault and battery to kill, and sentenced not for a term of years, but for safe keeping; he is a harmless imbecile. One was sent here from Luzerne county for ten years, on a charge of burglary and larceny. The object seemed to be, to rid the neighborhood of a troublesome fellow. One sent from Northampton county for ten years on charge of rape. One from Bradford county, charged with child murder, holding his own child under water, to see the effect of it, thus proving the insanity of the act; his sentence is twelve years. A woman from Luzerne county, for shooting her husband, sentenced to eleven years, and eleven months. She is very crazy, and not a fit subject for penitentiary discipline.

" One woman on several charges of larceny, sentenced to nine years. This woman has been an inmate of an insane asylum. One from Luzerne Co., for 'injury to rail road." He piled lumber on the road to see how it would be scattered by the engine (a crazy man's trick.) One from Philadelphia, for aggravated assault and battery, sentenced to seven years; very weak minded on admission, and easily provoked to violence. One from Philadelphia, for wife murder, sentence ten years; insane on admission. These individuals have received such care and attention as we were enabled to give them, but we have no accommodations for insane patients—*no* rooms larger than the ordinary cells. They have had such medical care as our resident physician was able to give them, but we have no suitable nurses, nor place for any. I consider it very improper, very unkind, very cruel, to send insane persons to a jail or penitentiary. It is almost certain to fasten the malady upon them, until it becomes irremediable. A hospital, with hospital appliances, is the only place for these poor stricken ones.

"I think that a hospital for the insane should not be connected in any way with a prison, but be entirely separate, and under separate administration.

"Could not a part of the Danville Asylum be thus used?

"Hoping these interrogatories are sufficiently answered, I remain, very truly and respectfully, thy friend,

"EDWARD TOWNSEND,
"*Warden.*"

REPORT OF WARDEN WRIGHT.

"ALLEGHENY, PA., *November* 24, 1873.

"GEO. L. HARRISON, ESQ.,

"President Board of Public Charities,

"Dear Sir.—In your letter of 17th of October, you request that I give you my views on the subject of the treatment of the criminal insane confined in penitentiaries and jails.

"The subject has often been referred to in the Annual Reports of this penitentiary, and the Inspectors in their report for 1844, say, 'If, in the present pecuniary embarrassment of the Commonwealth, you cannot erect and endow a State Asylum for the insane, we must urge upon you the propriety and necessity of authorizing us to establish, within the prison walls, a hospital, for the reception of the limited number of demented convicts which may unhappily come under our supervision. The occurrence is rare that they become so after they enter the penitentiary, but, in many instances, they are sent here after the commission of crime, because there is no other barrier to protect society from their demoniac depredations. There is a convict of this character now immured in one of our cells, for such is the sentence of the law. He came here in this lamentable condition.' In the report for 1857 it is said, ' convicts are often sent here whose proper destination should be the State Lunatic Hospital. Why they are sent here, whether for the purpose of supposed relief to the treasury of the county from which they come; from culpable ignorance of the law regulating the State Lunatic Asylum, or from the suggestion flattering to us, that we will take good care of them, and that society at large will be exempt from the dangers incident to a too close proximity to madmen; it is a practice alike contrary to the policy of the law, and the dictates of humanity.'

"I have thus far made up, as briefly as practicable, from our own reports evidence that insanity has proven no bar to conviction and confinement in the penitentiary, and do not doubt further evidence could be given showing that harmless imbecile prisoners, have been received and discharged without further record, than such as was given to other prisoners.

"As having a direct bearing upon the views expressed in a former report, that prisons are often used as asylums, the following extract from the report of the Warden of the Eastern Penitentiary for the year 1871, bears pertinent testimony, 'men are frequently sent to this penitentiary who are not fit subjects for its discipline. During the year four men were received who were quite insane when admitted; one in unsound mind; and four of weak intellect. One of these insane prisoners died of tetanus, resulting from injuries inflicted upon himself shortly after his reception, and another committed suicide in one month after he came here. Of the nine hundred and eleven confined in 1871, twelve were insane when admitted; four of unsound mind; two feeble minded and thirty-six of weak intellect, bordering on idiocy.'

"In the annual report of the Eastern Penitentiary for 1872 it is stated that two hundred and twenty-six convicts were received during the year, of whom one was of unsound mind, four were weak minded, fifteen were dull and two doubtful, making nearly ten per cent. of impaired intellect. Of the two hundred and seventeen convicts discharged, one insane, died, two were weak-minded and thirteen were dull, being nearly seven and a half per cent. of the discharged, impaired in intellect.

"Under the provisions of the Act of 1852, four prisoners were removed in December, 1859, of whom the physician of the prison states, 'It would be absurd to assert that no case of insanity ever occurred in this prison, but, to show the probable effect of the discipline in these cases, I will refer to their condition on admission:—No. 1419 general good health, but appears to be of unsound mind; circumstances had led to the belief of insanity, before he was brought to the prison. No. 1485 general good health. No. 1987 good health, but owing to his inability to speak English, his mental condition was not recognized, but I now have no doubt he was insane when admitted. No. 2094 insane.' One of the above noted prisoners, No. 1485, was returned to the prison exactly three months after his transfer to the hospital, of whom it is afterwards entered that he died in the prison, insane, in January, 1862, after an imprisonment of ten years and nine months. The physician notes in his official report, 'upon his return here, he was still decidedly insane.' [Dixmont Hospital was not then open.]

"The physician's record of insane prisoners as given to your Board and printed on page 14 of report for 1870, in brief, shows that one prisoner died in 1862, (previously noted as received in good health in 1851,) and seven others were received from 1863 to 1868, five were sent to Dixmont by order of the Governor, and two were discharged insane. All were insane or of feeble intellect when admitted.

"The physician notices eight cases of the various forms of insanity under treatment in 1871, who are stated to have been received insane; four were transferred from the Eastern Penitentiary; one had been in several insane asylums; one when received was a mental and physical wreck (since dead;) one had been held in jail a long time, owing to uncertainty is still confined, a complete imbecile; one had been mentally as to his mental health. He was sent to Dixmont where he impaired for several years. None of the cases originated in this prison. The report for 1872 contains further mention of the four cases remaining over from the preceding year.

"The records of jails and other institutions within the Commonwealth, if culled from the official reports to your Board, would furnish abundant evidence of the need for a change in the present method of treatment of the criminal insane.

"I doubt not you will recommend some important changes, and whether you favor the erection of a State Asylum for the 'Crimimal Insane,' or, endeavor to meet the present exigency, by procuring the setting apart of a wing in one or more of the existing State Lunatic Hospitals, I trust you will arrive at a satisfactory solution of this important question, and submit a plan wise in its details and ennobling in its humanity. Very respectfully,

"EDWARD S. WRIGHT,
" *Warden.*"

We pass now to the consideration of the third class of insane persons, viz., of those who having committed acts of violence or mischief, are acquitted of crime on the ground of insanity.

Here we presume that those persons who commit such acts under a partial aberration of mind, or a monomania, or a sudden impulse, which did not destroy or disable the power of rational, moral judgment; or under a temporary delirous excitement, resulting from their own deliberate action, and the cause of which was under their own control, as in a fit of intoxication, are

NOT TO BE REGARDED AS PROPERLY INSANE,

and should not be acquitted of crime on that ground. But acts committed in a state of proper insanity, that is to say,

WHEN THE WHOLE RATIONAL FACULTY IS SO DERANGED,

that the moral judgment, the power of discrimination between right and wrong, is, by the visitation of Providence, utterly blotted out or partially paralyzed; such acts, however destructive or atrocious, cannot, without great impropriety and even absurdity, be denominated crimes; and those who so commit them, cannot be classed among criminals. An "insane criminal," as an expression intended to describe a person as having committed a crime while in a state of insanity, is a contradiction in terms.

How the facts are to be ascertained in these cases or what are the proper evidences, is not a point which concerns us at present; such questions belong to courts, juries and experts; but *if* the facts have been ascertained and adjudicated; *if* there is admitted to have existed in the person arraigned, such a general mental derangement as obliterated the moral judgment, or any other mania which involved the loss or subversion of the moral judgment and control, in relation to those acts to which the impulse or propensity points, whether such be judged and found curable or incurable, and whether the lunatic be adjudged dangerous or harmless;—then

SUCH ACTS CANNOT BE RECKONED CRIMES,

and the person who has committed them cannot, without gross injustice and inhumanity, be regarded or treated as a criminal. And such is presumed to be the case of all those, who are acquitted of crime on the ground of insanity. Yet under our laws and the administration of justice (!) in this

Commonwealth, numbers of these innocent and pitiable sufferers *are* so regarded and treated,—especially those who are tainted with the sin of poverty, as well as the crime of insanity. This is, at the present moment, one of the

FOULEST BLOTS UPON THE ESCUTCHEON OF OUR STATE,

a blot, which, instead of being in process of gradual effacement, has been made darker and deeper by our more recent legislation. All the improvement and tendency to improvement in this respect, which resulted and promised to result from the just and merciful laws of 1845 and 1852, have been retracted and reversed by the law of 1861.

The cases of insanity to which we now refer may be variously classified, but the law fixes its attention chiefly on that form of mania, which is more or less dangerous, and requires more or less restraint for the protection of the community, as well as for the safety of the patient.

And that the case may be brought clearly and in one view under the eye of the members of the Legislature, we may be excused for here reciting somewhat at large the present provisions of our laws on this subject, as they stand in the statute book.

PROCEEDINGS AGAINST CRIMINAL LUNATICS.
ACT OF 1836.

[At the time this Act was passed there was no State Hospital for the insane, and for want of such institutions they were sent to the penitentiaries and jails.]

SECTION. 58. In every case in which it shall be given in evidence upon the trial of any person charged with any crime or misdemeanor, that such person was insane at the time of the commission of such offence, and such person shall be acquitted, the jury shall be required to find specially whether such person was insane at the time of the commission of such offence, and to declare whether such person was acquitted by them on the ground of such insanity, and if they shall so find and declare, the court before whom the trial was had, shall have power to order such person to be kept in strict custody, in such place and in such manner as to the said court shall seem fit, at the expense of the county in which the trial was had, so long as such person shall continue to be of unsound mind.

Sec. 59. The same proceedings may be had, if any person indicted for an offence shall, upon arraignment, be found to be a lunatic by a jury, lawfully impanelled for the purpose; or if upon the trial of any person so indicted, such person shall appear to the jury, charged with such indictment, to be a lunatic; in which case, the court shall direct such finding to be recorded, and may proceed as aforesaid.

Sec. 60. In every case in which any person, charged with any offence, shall be brought before the court, to be discharged for want of prosecution; and shall, by the oath or affirmation of one or more credible persons, appear to be insane, the court shall order the prosecuting attorney to send before the grand jury, a written allegation of such insanity, in the nature of a bill of indictment, and, thereupon the said grand jury shall make inquiry into the case, as in cases of crime, and make presentment of their finding to said court; and if said grand jury shall affirm said written allegation, they shall endorse the same thereon, and, thereupon, the court shall order a jury to be impanelled to try the insanity of such person. But before a trial thereof be ordered, the court shall direct notice thereof to be given to the next of kin of such person, by publication or otherwise, as the case may require. And if the jury shall find such person to be insane, the like proceedings may be had as aforesaid.

Sec. 61. *Provided*, That if the kindred or friends of any person, who may have been acquitted, as aforesaid, on the ground of insanity, or in default of such, the guardians, overseers, or supervisors of any county, township, or place, shall give security in such amount as shall be satisfactory to the court, with condition that such lunatic shall be restrained from the commission of any offence by seclusion or otherwise, in such case it shall be lawful for the court to make an order for the enlargement of such lunatic, and his delivery to his kindred or friends; or, as the case may be, to such guardian, overseers, or supervisors.

ACT APRIL 14TH, 1845.

SEC. 8. The admission of insane patients, from the several counties of the Commonwealth, shall be in the ratio of their insane population: Provided that each county shall be entitled to send at least one insane patient.

SEC. 9. Indigent persons and paupers shall be charged actual cost, &c., payable by counties.

SEC. 10. The courts of this Commonwealth shall have power to commit to said asylum, any person, who, having been charged with an offence punishable by imprisonment or death, who shall have been found to have been insane in the manner now provided by law, at the time the offence was committed, and who still continues insane, and the expenses of said person, if in indigent circumstances shall be paid by the county, &c.

Sec. 12. The several constituted authorities having care and charge of the poor of the respective counties, districts, and townships, shall have authority to send to the asylum, such insane paupers under their charge, as they may deem proper subjects, and they shall be severally chargeable with the expenses of the care, and maintenance, and removal to and from the asylum, of such paupers.

SEC. 14. That if any person shall apply to any court of record within this Commonwealth, having jurisdiction of offences, which are punishable by imprisonment, for the term of ninety days or longer, for the commitment to said asylum of any insane person within the county in which such court has jurisdiction, it shall be the duty of said court to inquire into the fact of insanity in the manner provided by law; and if such court shall be satisfied, that such person is, by reason of insanity, unsafe to be at large, or is suffering any unnecessary duress or hardship, such court, shall, on the application aforesaid, commit such insane person to said asylum.

SEC. 15. In the order of admission, the indigent insane of this Commonwealth, shall have always precedence of the rich (in another place "paying patients") and ——— recent cases shall have precedence of those of long standing.

ACT OF MAY 4TH, 1852.

Whenever in the opinion of the Inspectors of the Eastern Penitentiary, any of the prisoners therein confined, shall develop such marked insanity, as to render their continued confinement in said penitentiary improper, and their removal to the State Lunatic Hospital necessary to their restoration, it shall be the duty of the said Inspectors to submit such cases to a Board composed of the District Attorney of the county of Philadelphia, the principal physician of the Pennsylvania Hospital for the Insane, at Philadelphia, and the principal physician of the Friends' Insane Asylum, at Frankford, in Philadelphia County, and in case a majority of them cannot at any time, when required, attend, a competent physician, or physicians to be appointed by the Court of Quarter Sessions of the County of Philadelphia, in the place of such as cannot attend, upon whose certificate of insanity or the certificate of any two transmitted to the governor, and if by him approved, he shall direct that said insane prisoners, shall be, by said Inspectors, removed to the State Lunatic Hospital, there to be kept and properly provided for at the cost and charge of the county from which they were sent to the penitentiary, and if, at any time during the period for which any such insane prisoners shall have been sentenced to confinement in the Eastern Penitentiary, they shall in the opinion of the trustees of the said Lunatic Hospital be so far restored as to render their return to said penitentiary safe and proper, then the said trustees shall cause the said prisoner to be returned to said Eastern Penitentiary, due notice to be given to the clerk of the Court of Quarter Sessions of the county from which such prisoners were sent to the penitentiary, of all such removals or transfers.

ACT OF APRIL 8TH, 1861.

SEC. 1. When application shall be made under the 14th section of the Act of April 14, 1845, to which this is supplementary, to any court of this Commonwealth for the commitment of any person to the Pennsylvania State Lunatic Hospital, it shall be lawful for such court either to inquire into the fact of insanity in a summary way, &c.; and in all cases, it shall be lawful for the several courts to use their discretion in sending insane persons to said hospital, or cause them to be confined elsewhere, as the said court may deem the case to be curable or otherwise.

SEC. 2. No person shall hereafter be sent to the said Lunatic Hospital, under the 10th section of Act 14, April, 1845, or any other law of this Commonwealth, who shall have been charged with homicide, or having endeavored or attempted to commit the same, or to commit any arson, rape, robbery or burglary, and have been acquitted of any such offences on the ground of insanity, or been proceeded against under the 59th or 60th sections of the Act of 1836, [see above] where the court trying the same shall be satisfied that it will be dangerous for such lunatic to be at large, on account of having committed or attempted to commit either of the crimes aforesaid, but such persons shall be confined in a penitentiary or the prison of the proper county.

SEC. 3. In every case where a lunatic has been or shall be committed to said hospital, after an acquittal of any crime on the ground of insanity, or after an investigation in court under the 59th & 60th sections of the Act 13, June 1836, or on account of its being adjudged dangerous for such lunatic to be at large; and in all cases where any lunatic has been, or shall be removed from either of the penitentiaries, or any prison of this Commonwealth, under the order of a judge or of any court it shall be lawful for the trustees of said hospital with the aid of the superintending physician, to inquire carefully into the situation of the lunatic, and if a majority of the Board, including the physician, shall be satisfied that that there is no reasonable prospect of a cure of the insanity, being affected by a retention of the lunatic in the hospital they shall at the expense of the proper city or county, cause him or her, to be removed to the prison of the proper county or the penitentiary from which he or she was sent.

Thus it appears that before 1845,—before the erection of a State Lunatic Hospital, (1) persons tried and acquitted of crime on the ground of insanity, (2) persons indicted for an offence and found to be insane when brought up for trial, and (3) persons charged with some offence and brought before the court, to be discharged for want of prosecution, but being found in a state of lunacy,—provided they had no friends—were to be sent to the penitentiary, the county jail, or, if the county authorities should give the required guarantees, to the county poorhouse—as the court should judge most proper.

By the Act of 1845 and the establishment of the State Lunatic Hospital, this state of things was at once and in prospect greatly improved. This alleviation was obtained upon the Memorials of Miss Dix and other philanthropic citizens, backed by the following representation from the judges of the criminal courts:

The Memorial of Miss Dix to the Legislature, dated February 3d, 1845, contains the following certificate from members of the Judiciary in relation to the imprisonment of "insane criminals," Miss Dix prefacing its introduction with this paragraph:

"Next after private families and poorhouses, the insane will be found in the jails and penitentiaries. On this subject the opinion of some of your jurists has been so explicitly declared, that I feel it but justice to the cause, to give this expression of their sentiments place here."

"PHILADELPHIA, *March* 5, 1839.

"The want of an asylum for the insane poor often occasions painful embarrassments to the courts, when the defence in the criminal charge is insanity fully sustained by proof. Although the jury may certify that their acquittal is on that ground, and thus empower the court to order the prisoner into close custody, *yet that custody can be in no other place than the common prisons*, places illy qualified for such a subject of incarceration. We cannot doubt that the ends of justice would be greatly promoted, if such an asylum as the petitioners contemplated were established with proper regulations, and the courts were authorized to commit to it, all persons acquitted of crimes on the ground of insanity."

(Signed) EDWARD KING,
ARCHIBALD RANDALL,
J. RICHTER JONES,
Judges of the Court of Quarter Sessions·

JAMES TODD,
J. BOUVIER,
R. T. CONRAD,
Judges of the Criminal Sessions:

CALVIN BLYTHE,
Judge of the Twelfth Judicial District.

Miss DIX adds, "It is believed that all the judges of the courts of the Commonwealth of Pennsylvania, having criminal jurisdiction, would coincide in the above opinion."

But by the Act of 1861, now in force, the benefits which had been secured—which it was hoped would be secured, and which the judiciary thus earnestly desired might be secured, have been substantially annulled and frustrated:— for, as to the subsequent Act of April 20, 1869,—an Act intended to guard the commitment to, and secure a proper discharge from private hospitals,—it will be seen immediately, that they simply provide for the mode of procedure in one particular case, viz: in *discharging* a person who has been acquitted of crime on the ground of insanity, at the time of its commission, but who is alleged now to be sane. It provides for his "confinement," and then prescribes how the question of his sanity shall, before his discharge, be adjudicated. It is, in fact, legislation for the sane and not for the insane. [See Judge Brewster's "opinion" further on.]

Under the first section of this Act (of 1861) a person, a man or woman, though free from the taint or charge of any crime whatever, having committed no act of violence or mischief—a poor, pitiable, harmless lunatic,

MAY BE SENT TO A JAIL FOR INDEFINITE INCARCERATION;

and if, upon summary examination, such person is thought to be more probably incurable, it is more than suggested to be the DUTY of the court to send him to prison. And, if once sent there, his case is remediless, unless he can get through the provision of Sect. 3, and we shall see what probability there is of that.

Under the second section, no person charged with committing or attempting to commit certain heinous crimes, and acquitted of the charge on the ground of insanity, shall, if the court judge it dangerous to be at large, be sent to the hospital at all, but he

SHALL BE CONFINED IN THE PENITENTIARY OR THE PRISON OF THE PROPER COUNTY;

that is to say, the only option left to the court is, either at once to discharge such a person and let him go at large, or to commit him to a hopeless imprisonment—hopeless, we say, unless he can run the gauntlet of Sect. 3.

Under this third section—and this is the key to the right understanding of the present state of our whole legislation on this subject,—any lunatic who (1) upon trial, has been acquitted

OF ANY CRIME WHATEVER,

and however slight, or, (2) who has been indicted for *any offence*, and upon being brought up for trial, has been found insane, or, (3) who, when brought up to be discharged for want of prosecution, is found insane, or, (4) who, though *never charged* with any crime or any act of violence or harm, has been adjudged dangerous, if allowed to go at large,—any lunatic of either of these four classes, who has, thereupon been sent by the order of any court, to a State hospital for the insane,—as well as any lunatic (5) who by the order of the Governor or by any provision of law, has been removed from any penitentiary or jail to the said hospital, may, upon the judgment of the trustees and superintending physician, of said hospital, that there is no reasonable prospect of a cure of his insanity, be, by them, and by their sole and uncontrolled authority, consigned to a helpless and hopeless

IMPRISONMENT IN THE PENITENTIARY OR THE COUNTY JAIL.

(Perhaps we ought to remark by the way that the last words of the section, "from which he or she was sent," may seem to confine the exercise of the power of the hospital authorities to the fifth class of persons before described; but as, in that case the four other classes would have been enumerated in the section without any enactment in regard to them, it is presumed the Act should be interpreted as extending the same power of removing the parties from the hospital to prison, to all those four classes of cases also ; and so we believe it has always been interpreted. But, perhaps it is to the credit of those who drew the Act, that that there should be marks of *haste* in its composition.) It is clear, however, that this act contains no authority for sending any patients, however incurable, to the county poorhouses; they can be sent back only to the prison or the penitentiary.

We must ask your indulgence, gentlemen of the Legislature, if we find ourselves compelled to speak harshly, or even disrespectfully, of the law of the land. We are addressing legislators and not a jury. But what a law is this! Is it possible that the members of our subsequent legislatures—is it possible that you, gentlemen, have been fully aware of its extraordinary, of its atrocious provisions! a law, which we are constrained to say, in the terrible coolness of its barbarous enactments—in its disregard not only of all the claims of humanity and justice, but of the simplest civil rights of every citizen, is, so far as we can find, without a parallel in the legislation of any other State of this Union, or of any Christian or civilized community in the world. By this law, not only are persons—men and women, who are admitted and solemnly adjudged to be innocent of all crime,—men and women, who have never even been charged with any act of violence or harm,—liable to be hopelessly incarcerated—incarcerated professedly for life; (for they are pronounced *probably incurable*,—and this is their only crime,) incarcerated in the common jail or the penitentiary,—incarcerated in the society of felons,—incarcerated where they can have no proper care or treatment;— not only this—but such persons liable to be so incarcerated, not upon the verdict of a jury of their fellow citizens, or the examination and sentence of any court of justice, but upon the dictum—the sole, peremptory, uncontrolled and irreversible dictum—of whom?

THE DICTUM OF THE TRUSTEES AND SUPERINTENDING PHYSICIAN OF A STATE HOSPITAL!

a tribunal unknown, elsewhere, to the constitution and laws of the State; whose rescript overrides and reverses the solemn sentences of all the criminal courts of the Commonwealth; and holds, in respect to them, the character of a judgment of a Supreme Court of Errors and Appeals; and the *appeal* to this court is made by the court itself:—and even this is not all; but the court is the party interested to be rid of the care and burden of the poor speechless and defenceless victims, whose cases are to be passed upon!

Can anything be added to the extraordinary character of such a law? Shall it be allowed any longer to disgrace our statute book, and tarnish the fair fame of our beloved and honored State?

No man, no one of us, gentlemen, can be sure that he will not become a helpless lunatic to-morrow. But does every citizen of Pennsylvania know that he is liable, without any fault of his own, to be sent at any time to the common jail for life long detention, by the sole and irrevokable authority and sentence of the superintendent and trustees of a State Lunatic Hospital? And that in spite of, and reversal of, the contrary judgment and sentence of any and every court of justice, which may have passed, or which by law can pass upon his case.

We beg here to disclaim, once for all, intending any personal reference to or reflection upon the estimable gentlemen who have the charge of the State Hospitals for the insane. We doubt not they are honorable and conscientious men; but they are *men.* The constitution of such a court of review must, we think, be admitted to be

AN ANOMALY IN OUR LEGISLATION,

and no less an anomaly that interested parties, however honorable and trustworthy, should be empowered to decide in their own case. And perhaps it is worth observing that, while a lunatic may be thus summarily removed from the hospital to the prison, by the simple fiat of the hospital authorities alone, a lunatic could not so readily be removed from the penitentiary to the hospital. For this purpose the law of 1852 presented a complex process. In order that a lunatic might be removed from the penitentiary to the hospital, the law provided that not only the inspectors of the penitentiary —honorable and conscientious men—should judge the continued confinement of such lunatic in the penitentiary to be improper, and his removal to the State Lunatic Asylum necessary to his restoration, but the case must also be submitted to a board composed of the District Attorney and either two superintendents of insane asylums or a competent physician or physicians to be appointed by the Court of

Quarter Sessions. Nor was their certificate of approval sufficient to secure the object: but that certificate must be transmitted to the Governor, and, if he approved, he might order the removal. So careful was the law in that case to guard the process against abuse.

But we may be asked why we should cavil at what may be considered a theoretic anomaly, while it accomplishes the best results, and is the shortest and best way of accomplishing them? We answer by asking in return,

WHAT HAVE BEEN THE RESULTS?

Have the courts, by them, been encouraged to send lunatics to the hospital, or, on the contrary, have they found that this is too often a roundabout way of sending them to prison? But why is it that for more than twenty years the law has existed for sending certian lunatics from the penitentiaries to the hospital, and yet the experiment of doing so has been tried in the Eastern District of the State but once—indeed has not been tried at all in that district, for full twenty years past? Is it said that the lunatics so transmitted very soon made their escape? But if the hospital is by law to receive such lunatics, some part of it ought manifestly to be so constructed and arranged as to be suitable for their safe-keeping; as has been done without difficulty or opposition in the hospitals of several other States. Have the hospital authorities sought to provide such construction and arrangements, in order that the ends of the law might not be defeated? Or, have they not rather sought and obtained the counter provisions of the law of 1861, authorizing them to send all such lunatics back to prison? Since which time it has been hardly thought worth while to commit any such to their care. Indeed it has been triumphantly said, on apparently good authority, (see Journal of Insanity, Oct. 1873, page 214) that, after the first experiment, *i. e.* before the law of 1861, as well as since, the Board of Trustees of the State Lunatic Hospital at Harrisburg declined receiving any more cases." That is to say, the Board of Trustees decided the question by their *sole* and ultimate authority—commission or no commission—law or no law. We do not vouch for the fact, but it has been publicly so stated, without dissent, in the presence of the Superintendent of the Lunatic Asylum. We presume the refusal, if made, was a mere declaration and not an act; but the statement, however interpreted, is highly suggestive. The Act of 1852 is still the law of the land—a law whose ends are eminently politic, just and humane, but can the authorities of the State Hospital be counted upon as ready cordially to concur in carrying out the provisions of that law, for the accomplishment of those ends?

The views of the judges of our criminal courts and of the Supreme Court of the State, upon present legislation in regard to the insane poor and the insane criminal will appear in their petitions to the Legislature, which we here introduce:

TO THE LEGISLATURE OF THE STATE OF PENNSYLVANIA.

"The judges of the criminal courts being greatly embarrassed under the law of 1836, in the disposal of persons charged with crime, who were acquitted on the ground of insanity, being obliged to commit them to 'close custody;' the jails and penitentiaries being alone open to them, memorialized the Legislature in 1839, in behalf of the establishment of a hospital for the 'insane poor,' and denounced the commitment of the irresponsible insane to the prisons of the State. By such influence and other humane and rightful effort, the Legislature, in 1845, established the State Lunatic Hospital at Harrisburg, under a law which gave proper protection to the rights of the 'poor' and the 'criminal insane.' This legislation satisfied the judges who bore the responsibility of disposing of such persons, and was also a clear exponent of the public mind on the subject.

"By more recent legislation, namely by the Act of April 8th, 1861, the courts, having jurisdiction of such cases, are forbidden to send them to the State hospitals, however irresponsible for crime, unless 'speedily curable,' *if they are deemed dangerous persons to be at large;* and in every case where a lunatic may have been sent to the State Hospital, *after an acquittal of any crime on the ground of insanity*, the authorities of such hospital *may send such persons to a penitentiary or jail*, at the expense of the county where he belongs, unless they deem the case 'speedily curable.' Substantially the same provisions are contained in the Act of April, 1863, relating to the western part of the State. The undersigned, regarding the provisions of the Acts of 1861 and 1863, above cited, as an obstruction to the ends of justice; and, being greatly embarrassed in our administration of such causes, respectfully beg that the legislation be repealed, or such amendments made, as will relieve from unjust and injurious imprisonment with felons, the irresponsible class referred to, and which will also protect the 'insane poor' in their rights, and enable the courts to comply with the laws, without violating a sense of right or a sentiment of humanity.

"The Act of April, 1863, in relation to the commitment of the insane to the Western Pennsylvania Hospital provides for the return of insane criminals and persons acquitted on the ground of insanity, to the jail or penitentiary if deemed incurable."

JOS. ALLISON,
JAS. R. LUDLOW,
WM. S. PEIRCE,
THOS. A. FINLETTER,
EDWARD M. PAXSON,
Judges of Court of Quarter Sessions, Philadelphia Co.

F. H. COLLIER,
JAMES P. STERRETT,
EDWIN H. STOWE,
Judges of Court of Quarter Sessions of Allegheny Co.

"We concur in the above recommendation,"

GEO. SHARSWOOD,
HENRY W. WILLIAMS,
JOHN M. READ.
DANIEL AGNEW,
ULYSSES MERCUR.
Judges of Supreme Court.

Nov. 28th, 1873.

We turn to another description of the insane—to those, who without any charge or suggestion of crime, have, either as dangerous or simply as helpless lunatics, been placed in the county poorhouses. These may by law be committed by the county authorities to the State hospitals for the insane—How many of them have been so committed? Does the management of these hospitals encourage and stimulate the authorities to send them there?

THEY NEED ENCOURAGEMENT AND STIMULUS;

for, as experience too constantly shows, those authorities are extremely liable to be led by the considerations of a false and short-sighted economy, to endeavor to make a cheaper provision for the care and maintenance of their insane, than that furnished by the hospital. Are those whom they actually commit, sent back to them again, with a charge for the expense of both transfers? If so,

BY THE AUTHORITY OF WHAT LAW ARE THEY SENT BACK?

What law provides that the authorities of the hospitals may send any of their patients, or allow any of their patients, however violent or incurable, to be taken to a county poorhouse? Yet the simple fact is that while there are some five hundred of the insane poor, in our hospitals, sent from the county almhouses, there are more than twice that number

RAVING OR LANGUISHING IN OUR COUNTY POORHOUSES,

an incarceration much better fitted to make a sane man mad, than a madman sane. And of the two, if there is less disgrace, there is also, in a majority of cases, less chance for comfort, and no better chance for recovery, in the poorhouse than in the prison. So that it may be said upon a deliberate calculation, to be better, as regards comfort and a prospect of restoration,

FOR AN INSANE PERSON TO BE CONVICTED OF CRIME,

and sentenced to the penitentiary for a definite time, than, as an innocent lunatic, to be imprisoned in the poorhouse.

But, we may add that the great and irremediable defect in both the prison and the poorhouse, but especially in the latter, is the want of proper attendance, and of skillful medical care. These poor creatures are not expected to recover. They are given over to utter hopelessness.

And now,

WHAT IS TO BE DONE?

To this question we would address ourselves with the full appreciation of the many and formidable difficulties with which the subject is encompassed. But we believe that there is no thoughtful person, who has made himself practically acquainted with the facts, that does not fully concur in the judgment that no poorhouse can be a proper receptacle for the insane. We shall enter into no argument, therefore, to show that

ALL THE INSANE POOR

now gathered in the county poorhouses should, as soon as possible, be provided for in State lunatic hospitals, and transferred to them, to be there supported as the law may direct, unless any particular county has population enough, and insane poor enough, to render it advisable and feasible to establish and maintain a separate hospital for itself, with the full appointments and provisions for the best and most skillful care and medical treatment of the inmates, with a view both to their comfort and their care, as well as to the safety of the community.

As to the other less numerous class, who have been committed by the courts (or by the hospital authorities) to the jails or the penitentiaries; including (1) those who, having been charged with the most heinous felonies, have been acquitted on the ground of insanity, (2) those who, on the same ground, have been acquitted of any offence whatever and however slight, (3) those who have been indicted for any offence, and upon being brought up for trial, have been found insane; (4) those, who, when brought up to be discharged for want of prosecution, have been found insane;

(5) those, who, though never charged with any act of crime or harm whatever, have been judged dangerous if allowed to go at large; as well as (6) those who, having been convicted of crime, committed while they were presumed to be sane, have since become lunatics,—in regard to all these, it seems now to be universally conceded that,

THE JAIL OR THE PENITENTIARY IS NOT THE PROPER PLACE FOR THE KEEPING OR CARE OF SUCH LUNATICS.

The practical question then is what other provision is to be made for them?

The Act of May 4, 1852, had, as we have seen, provided that any of the prisoners confined in the Eastern Penitentiary, being found insane (thus, insane convicts as well, but not insane convicts only) might, by a certain process, be removed to the State Lunatic Asylum. In their report of the year following, the Inspectors of the Penitentiary inform us, that of eighteen persons proposed by them as candidates for removal, eight had been so transferred by order of the Governor, and they add:

"The Inspectors cannot omit this opportunity of again calling upon the General Assembly, should the means provided for this object be found in any way inadequate, either in the terms of the law authorizing the removal, or in the provision for the safe-keeping in the lunatic hospital, not to halt in the good work until it is carried into full effect. Let it no longer rest upon the fair fame of Pennsylvania, who claims to be foremost in the work of penitentiary reforms, that insane men are imprisoned in the cells of her penitentiary for long years or for life. . . . Surely in this enlightened Christian age and country, the cells of the penitentiary should cease to be the abode of human beings without moral perceptions or responsibilities to fit them for the salutary effects of either penitentiary punishments or moral reform. The inspectors have gone more fully into this subject than they otherwise would have done, from the fact that a state hospital has been been put into operation by the Legislature for this enlightened and benevolent purpose. Its establment has been long needed."

In their report for the next year (1854) the Inspectors remark that "the eight persons before alluded to, were the first so removed since the opening of the prison twenty-five years ago, as until last year no institution existed in Pennsylvania, as in other States, for the reception and treatment of persons, who, though insane, required punitive restraint. No other cases have since occurred requiring removal from the penitentiary. The State Lunatic Hospital is an establishment of the highest utility,—its purpose approved by the most enlightened benevolence and sound policy. Every humane mind cannot but hope that it it will be fostered and encouraged for the accomplishment of benefits to an increasing class of unfortunate people." They then proceed to a class who are sometimes included among the "criminal insane," in the following terms:—" As yet no complete provisions have been made for the reception and treatment of those insane who are sentenced to restraint of their liberty, because the fact of their unsound mind renders them irresponsible for the crimes charged against them. There are now four prisoners in the penitentiary thus confined; their dangerous character, arising from homicidal mania, rendering them unsafe, unless under a cautious restraint. As they are in the penitentiary not as convicts, but here retained because of no other place of equal security, it is difficult properly to treat them for the confirmed malady under which they labor. The time will come when in the State Hospital, provision can be made for this class of insane."

Nearly twenty years have elapsed, and these poor, wretched beings are still in jails and almshouses.

The inspectors making the report in 1853, were John Bacon, Richard Vaux, Hugh Campbell, Singleton A. Mercer and Charles Brown; in 1854, Messrs. Bacon, Vaux, Mercer, Andrew Miller and Charles McKibben.

Then came the law of 1861; which empowers the trustees and physician of the State Lunatic Hospital to send insane persons committed to the hospital by the courts or removed to it from the penitentiary, back to the penitentiary from which they were sent, or to a prison to which they were not committed by the courts, when there appeared no reasonable prospect of a cure. The result is that it is found a useless expenditure of pains and money, in many cases, for the courts to send to the hospitals insane men acquitted of crime, and always for the penitentiary to remove thither its prisoners or insane convicts, while authority resides in the hospital to forthwith send them back again. In anticipation of this result, the inspectors of the Eastern Penitentiary, in their report of the following year (1862,) "respectfully suggest to the Legislature that provision by law be made *requiring the State Lunatic Asylum to take insane persons convicted of crime into that institution.*" And, in 1863, "the inspectors again ask the Legislature to require the State Lunatic Asylum to take 'insane convicts.'" The inspectors in 1862 and 1863 were Richard Vaux, Samuel Jones, M. D., Alexander Henry, Thomas H. Powers and Furman Sheppard.

It is plain that these gentlemen, as well as the Inspectors of 1853 and 1854, judged it to be the wisest and most desirable plan, in this as in other States, that provision should be made for the criminal insane and even for insane convicts IN CONNECTION WITH THE STATE HOSPITAL RATHER THAN WITH THE STATE PENITENTIARY.

We append here, without comment as the documents tell their own story very clearly, the communications to this Board from the Inspectors of the Eastern and Western Penitentiaries requesting its intervention with the Legislature, for the modification or repeal of the obnoxious laws against the rights of the insane, which now disgrace our statute books.

November 26th, 1873.

" TO THE BOARD OF PUBLIC CHARITIES :

" The Inspectors of the State Penitentiary for the Eastern District of Pennsylvania have heretofore in their reports called the attention of the Legislature to the deplorable condition of the insane committed to the custody of that Institution, and have suggested legislation which would relieve us from the pressure of a duty which we could not fulfil in providing for them proper care and medical treatment—and, which also would provide for these defenceless, and, for the most part, irresponsible, persons, a more rightful and suitable abode than a prison. We now most respectfully appeal to the Legislature, through your Board, to so amend the legislation of the Act of April 8, 1861, as will give effect to the former representations of the Inspectors, and place the class of the 'poor insane' and the 'criminal insane' in the more just and favorable position which they occupied under the law of April 14, 1845, which established the State Lunatic Asylum at Harrisburg."

RICHARD VAUX,
THOMAS H. POWERS,
ALEX. HENRY,
CHARLES THOMSON JONES,
JOHN M. MARIS.

"To THE BOARD OF PUBLIC CHARITIES:

"The Inspectors of the Western Penitentiary, desire to call the attention of the Legislature, through your Board, to the necessity of further and fuller provision by law, for the care and protection of the indigent and criminal insane.

"In many of the annual reports of this Penitentiary, attention has been directed to the fact, that insane persons have been convicted of crime and sent to prison. The following, from our report for 1867, briefly states the facts in the case, and in its conclusions, we trust, will receive your earnest co-operation.

"We would ask the attention of the Legislature to the great necessity there is for such legislation as will secure to the insane convict a place in some State institution where he may be properly cared for. By special amended enactments of the law on this subject, no insane convict, who has been committed to prison on the higher grades of crime, can be transferred to the hospital at Dixmont, 'unless by the verdict of the jury in the case there is reason to believe that a cure of such insanity may be speedily effected.'

"If this institution is intended only for the benefit of the *curably* insane, what is to become of the ill fated wretch who has no helper, and whose reason is declared to be '· clean gone forever.'

"We hold that it is the duty of the State to make some speedy provision for his relief, either by the modification of existing laws, or the enactment of such statutes as will guarantee to him a humane and Christian protection."

T. H. NEVIN,
ROBERT H. DAVIS,
JOHN DEAN,
GEORGE A. KELLY,
ORMSBY PHILLIPS,
Inspectors.

In like manner the Secretary of the Massachusetts Board of State Charities, in his report for 1871, recommends, and in that for 1872 renews the recommendation, that a special " receptacle or institution be provided for insane convicts, and for insane persons, who, in a state of insanity, have committed or are disposed to commit violent acts;" for which he gives his reasons at large, and then adds, "it is submitted that the construction of such a receptacle may perhaps be wisely made a part of the plan for a new hospital at Worcester. It can be made a separate building, surrounded by a wall, sufficiently removed from other buildings to avoid any unpleasant associations, and yet near enough to have the benefit of the general superintendence of that institution."

That is to say, as the Secretary immediately adds, the project of a new and (totally) separate institution for the class referred to, is sure to start some vexed question, with which it would not be well to embarrass the desired improvement. The "convict insane" would give to it its distinctive character; and then any proposition to admit to it others, not "convict insane," who could be better provided for in it, than elsewhere, would be resisted, as affixing to them the repute of a criminal class. Nor is it likely that it would, with its peculiar character, as well as its smaller numbers, be provided, in the long run, with a corps of officers equal in skill to those whose services are commanded by the other hospitals. For these and other reasons, it is better that provision should be made for the insane, who have committed or are pre-disposed to homicidal or violent acts, in buildings or apartments, properly arranged and provided with means of security,

IN CONNECTION WITH SOME ONE OF THE LUNATIC HOSPITALS."

So much from the secretary. The Board itself, in its first report, had said, "There is still another class, the 'criminal insane,' for whom special provision should be made. Formerly they were kept at the prisons, confined in cells; but more recently they have been placed in the State hospitals. It is generally thought that this class of the insane should not be allowed to mingle with those who are free from crime, but should have apartments built expressly for their accommodation. The most appropriate plan for an asylum, designed for this class of insane persons, would probably be

AT ONE OF THE STATE HOSPITALS."

The same subject was again referred to in their 5th & 6th reports; and again it is added, if a proper building for "insane convicts" and others predisposed to violent acts should be provided *in connection with one of the State Lunatic Hospitals*, power should be given to this Board, to transfer from the other hospitals to the one where such provision is made, persons of the class referred to. "From the other hospitals," observe—not, "from the prisons;,, in Massachusetts there are no "insane criminals," nor "insane convicts" in the prisons.

We have referred to the injurious and wrongful effects of the Act of 1861, and we have seen the earnest counter-recommendations of the Inspectors of the Eastern Penitentiary and other just and honorable authorities. We have, ourselves, already pointed out

THE DISASTROUS CONSEQUENCES OF THAT ACT;

and now, to confirm our position, we beg leave to insert here the results of the experience and research, and the carefully drawn statements, of Judge Brewster, on this point, conveyed to us in a letter dated October 10, 1873.

"No. 214 West Washington Square.
"Philadelphia, *October*, 10, 1873.
"To Hon. Geo. L. Harrison,
" *President of the Board of Public Charities,*
"Dear Sir:
"Your communication of August 14, in reference to 'insane criminals' was duly received and acknowledged.

"With your permission the examination of the authorities which you desired was postponed until a recent date.

"I have considered with some care the question you propound, and the several Acts of Assembly to which you referred me. I was induced to do this not only because of the respect due to your letter—but also because of the peculiar interest which ever attaches to the subject of the treatment of persons afflicted with the peculiar and distressing calamity of insanity.

"Your favor refers me to a passage which is to be found in a communication addressed by your Board to the public.

"As you invite a statement of my opinion as to its accuracy, it is proper that I should quote it at length—it is in these words:—

"'The sad and anomalous condition of 'insane criminals' 'under the provisions of the Act of 1836 relating to this 'class, did not satisfy the public mind little as the public

'mind takes cognizance of such matters, and it found in
'Miss Dix such an exponent of its wishes, as led to the leg-
'islation of 1845, which established the State Lunatic Hos-
'pital at Harrisburg, at which provision was made for the
'reception of this class of the insane, in community with
'the other patients. So largely did this feature interest the
'public that it was the common thought that this Institu-
'tion was created for the special care of this class. The
'Act of 1861 practically nullified this legislation and since
'then, a great wrong has been imposed upon them, which
'this Board is endeavoring to remove. Very many of
'them are consigned to the public jails. While wholly ir-
'responsible in the eyes of the law, they are dealt with by
'the law, as convicted criminals. We maintain that under
'the law of 1861, the wisdom and humanity of our able and
'excellent judges are not competent to make any other dis-
'position of them."'

"You ask me to give my 'professional opinion upon the
'accuracy of the statement' just quoted.

"Save for your request, which implies that some one has
ventured to doubt the correctnesss of your narrative, I should
not have supposed it possible that it needed confirmation.

"My first impression was decidedly in favor of its entire
truth and my subsequent examination of the law has confirmed my original conviction.

"By the Act of June 13, 1836, it was provided that upon
the acquittal of a defendant in a criminal case 'upon the
ground of insanity,' the court should have the 'power to
'order such person to be kept in strict custody in such place
'and in such manner as * * * * * should seem fit * * so long
'as such person should continue to be of unsound mind.'
(Act of June 13, 1836, § 58, P. L. 1836, page 603.

"The like proceedings were authorized if the defendant
were upon arraignment found to be a lunatic and even where
he was about to be discharged for want of prosecution.

"Prior to 1841 there was no place in which such unfortunate persons could be 'kept in strict custody, except prisons

and penitentairies. The private asylums were evidently not contemplated by the law, and were probably under no obligation to receive any person sent to them by the courts.

"March 4, 1841, Governor Porter approved an Act 'to 'establish an asylum for the insane of this Commonwealth.' This statute reflects great credit upon the gentleman who drafted it, and upon the Legislature and the Governor who passed and approved of it. It established "a public asylum for 'the reception and relief of the insane of this Commonwealth.' The Governor was to appoint three commissioners to purchase a site and to erect a building for the accommodation of 300 patients and necessary offices, at an expense not exceeding $120,000.

"The 8th section of said Act was designed to remedy the evil you refer to as existing under the statute of 1836. It provided:—

"'That the proper courts of this Commonwealth shall 'have power to commit to said asylum, any person who 'having been charged with an offence punishable by im-'prisonment or death, shall have been declared by the ver-'dict of a jury or otherwise, to the satisfaction of the court, 'to have been insane at the time the offence was committed, , and who still continues insane.'

"The prior Act of 1751 had contained no such provision. The Act of 1841 removed the blot upon our system of confining insane persons as criminals.

"So far as I have been able to discover, there was no change in this system for many years. It evidently met with the support of the people. By Act approved by Governor Shunk, April 14, 1845, a hospital was established at Harrisburg (P. L. 1845 p. 442.)

"The 10th section of this statute repeats the humane provision of the Act of 1841.

"March 18, 1848, Governor Shunk appoved the Act incorporating the Pittsburg Hospital. (P. L. 1848, p. 218.) By a supplement to this charter approved by Governor Pollock, May 8, 1855 (P. L.1855 p. 512) the provisions of the Act of 1841 were extended to that institution.

"Provisions for the removal of insane persons from prisons and penitentiaries to insane asylums were repeated by the Acts of May 4th, 1852 (P. L. 1852, p. 552,) and March 24th, 1858 (P. L. 1858, page 151.)

"So the law stood from 1841 to 1861. During those twenty years, the courts and all classes of citizens were satisfied with the propriety, justice and necessity of these laws.

"April 8, 1861, a statute was approved which prohibited the commitment to the Pennsylvania State Lunatic Asylum of any person charged with certain crimes therein enumerated. It, however, contained a humane proviso which left the power of commitment with the courts where they were satisfied that there was 'reason to believe that a cure of the insanity might be speedily effected' (P. L. 1861, page 249.) But a subsequent section authorizes the trustees and the superintending physician to reverse the order of the court, for if they are satisfied 'that there is no reasonable prospect of a 'cure' * * 'they may in all cases cause the patient to be re-'moved to the prison of the proper county or the penitentiary 'from which he or she was sent.'

"It is, therefore, unfortunately true as stated by you, that the Act of 1861 practically nullifies the humane legislation of former years, and that since 1861 a great wrong has been imposed upon a class of unfortunate persons who although not responsible to the law, are yet subject to confinement in prisons and penitentiaries as felons. These views are not affected in any wise by the Act of April 20, 1869, (P. L. 78) for the officers of the State asylums are not embraced within its provisions. The Act of 1861 stands unrepealed.

I am, very respectfully yours,

"F. CARROLL BREWSTER."

In a large number of our sister States, constitutional provision has been made to secure appropriate legislation in behalf of the insane; but in order to bring the whole subject more fully before the Legislature, in all its bearings, or, at least, in a great variety of points of view, we take leave to introduce here the legislative provisions of a number of States as to insane persons, charged or convicted of crime; premising that we have examined the constitutions and laws, together, of thirty-three States (all that we have been able to reach,) in relation to the insane, and in all cases their rights have been tenderly protected—and the legislation in behalf of the class to which we are now directing your attention, with the single exception of Pennsylvania, is invariably of the most humane character.

LEGISLATION OF OTHER STATES IN RELATION TO INSANE CRIMINALS.

ARKANSAS.

A person that becomes insane or lunatic after the commission of a crime or misdemeanor, shall not be tried for the offence during the insanity or lunacy.

If, after verdict of guilty and before judgment pronounced, such person becomes insane or lunatic, then no judgment shall be given while the insanity or lunacy shall continue.

If, after judgment and before execution of the sentence such convict becomes insane or lunatic, if the punishment be capital or corporal, the execution thereof shall be stayed until the recovery of such convict from such insanity or lunacy.

CONNECTICUT.

That section two hundred and forty-three of the Act concerning crimes and misdemeanors be amended by erasing from the fourth line thereof the words the "common jail" and inserting in lieu thereof the words "the General Hospital for the insane of the State of Connecticut."

GEORGIA.

It shall be the duty of the physician to the penitentiary of this State, when he discovers that any one of the convicts in said penitentiary has become lunatic or insane, to certify the same to the principal keeper of said penitentiary, and it shall be the duty of said principal keeper, upon the receipt of such certificate, to transfer said convict to the lunatic asylum of this State, and shall send together with such convict a copy of said certificate, together with the day on which the term of service of such convict will expire in said penitentiary, and the county from which he was sentenced.

LOUISIANA.

Whenever any person arrested to answer for any crime or misdemeanor before any court of this State, shall be acquitted thereof by the jury, or shall not be indicted by the grand jury, by reason of the insanity or mental derangement of such person, and the discharge or going at large of such person, shall be deemed by the court to be dangerous to the safety of the citizens or to the peace of the State, the court is authorized and empowered to commit such person to the State Insane Hospital or any similar institution in any parish within the jurisdiction of the court: There to be detained until he is restored to his right mind or otherwise delivered by due course of law.

MAINE.

When any person is indicted for a criminal offence, or is committed to jail on a charge thereof by a justice of the peace or judge of a police or municipal court, any judge of the court before which he is to be tried when a plea of insanity is made in court, or he is notified that it will be made, may in vacation or term time order such person into the care of the superintendent of the insane hospital, to be detained and observed by him till the further order of the court, that the truth or falsity of the plea may be ascertained.

When the grand jury omits to find an indictment against any person arrested by legal process to answer for any offence by reason of his insanity, they shall certify that fact to the court; and when a traverse jury for the same reason acquits any person indicted, they shall state that fact to the court when they return their verdict; and the court by a precept stating the fact of insanity, may commit him to prison or to the insane hospital till restored to his right mind or delivered according to law; *but he shall only remain in prison till provision can be made for him at the hospital and then removed thereto.*

When an inmate of the State prison becomes insane, the warden shall notify the Governor of the fact and he, with the advice of counsel, shall appoint a commission of two or more skillful physicians to investigate the case, and if such inmate is found insane by their investigation, he shall be sent to the insane hospital until he becomes of sound mind; and if this takes place before the expiration of his sentence, he shall be returned to prison; but if after, he shall be discharged free. The expenses of the commission, removal, and support shall be paid by the State.

MINNESOTA AND WISCONSIN.

When any person, indicted or informed against for an offence, shall on trial be acquitted by the jury, by reason of insanity, the jury in giving their verdict of not guilty, shall state that is was given for such cause, and thereupon if the discharge or going at large of such insane person shall be considered by the court manifestly dangerous to the peace and safety of the community, the court may order him to be committed to prison, or may give him into the care of his friends, if they shall give bonds with surety, to the satisfaction of the court, conditioned that he shall be well and securely kept; otherwise he shall be discharged.

OREGON.

If the defence be the insanity of the defendant, the jury must be instructed if they find him not guilty on that ground, to state that fact in their verdict, and the court must thereupon, if it deems his being at large dangerous to the public peace or safety, order him to be committed to any lunatic asylum authorized by the State to receive and keep such persons, until he become sane or be otherwise discharged therefrom, by authority of law. General laws Oregon, page 469 § 170.

NEW JERSEY AND NEW YORK.

When a person shall have escaped indictment or have been acquitted of a criminal charge upon trial, on the ground of insanity, upon the plea pleaded of insanity or otherwise, the court being certified by the jury or otherwise of the fact, shall carefully inquire and ascertain whether his insanity in any degree continues, and if it does, shall order him into safe custody, and to be sent to the asylum.

If any person in confinement, under indictment or under sentence of imprisonment, or for want of bail for good behavior * * shall appear to be insane, the judge of the circuit court of the county where he is confined shall institute a careful investigation, call two respectable witnesses, physicians and other credible witnesses, invite the prosecutor of the pleas to aid in the examination, and if he shall deem it necessary, call a jury, and for that purpose is fully empowered to compel the attendance of witnesses and jurors, and if it be satisfactorily proved that he is insane, said judge may discharge him from imprisonment, and order his safe custody, and removal to the asylum, where he shall remain until restored to his right mind, and then if the said judge shall have so directed, the superintendent shall inform the said judge and the county clerk and prosecutor of the pleas thereof, whereupon he shall be remanded to prison, and criminal proceedings be resumed, or otherwise be discharged.

Persons charged with misdemeanors, and acquitted on the ground of insanity, may be kept in custody and sent to the asylum in the same way as persons charged with crimes.

NEW YORK.

An Act to organize the State Lunatic Asylum for insane convicts, passed April 8th, 1858.

SEC. 1. The building now being erected on the prison grounds at Auburn, for an asylum for insane convicts, shall be known and designated as the "State Lunatic Asylum for insane convicts."

[After defining the method of administration, the statute proceeds;]

SEC. 8. Whenever the physicians of either of the State prisoners of this State shall certify to the inspectors, that any convict is insane, they shall make immediately a full examination into the condition of such convict, and shall cause such convict to be examined by one of the physicians of the State Lunatic Asylum at Utica, and if satisfied that the said convict is insane, or that there is probable cause to believe such convict to be insane, they shall order the agent and warden of the prison where such convict confined, forthwith to convey such convict to the State Lunatic Asylum for insane convicts, and to deliver the said convict to the superintendent thereof, who is hereby required to receive said convict into the said asylum, and retain him there so long as he shall continue to be insane, and no convict who has been committed to said asylum as insane, shall be discharged from said asylum by reason of the expiration of the term for which he was sentenced, unless the relatives of such convict shall produce to said superintendent satisfactory evidence of their ability to maintain such convict, and shall execute and deliver to said superintendent an agreement in writing that such convict shall not be a charge upon any public charity, if such convict shall continue to be insane at the expiration of the time for which such convict was sentenced.

ACT OF MAY 21, 1873.

No person, association or corporation shall establish or keep any asylum, institution, house of retreat for the care, custody or treatment of the insane, or persons of unsound mind, without first obtaining a license therefor from the Board of State Charities; *provided*, that this section shall not apply to any State asylum or institution, or to any asylum or institution established or conducted by any county or by any city or municipal corporation.

The said Board may revoke the license of any asylum or institution, issued under the provisions of this Act, for reasons deemed satisfactory to said board; but such revocation shall be in writing and filed, and notice given in writing to the person, association or corporation to whom such license was given.

ACT OF JUNE 7, 1873.

If any inmate of any such almshouse, when admitted, is insane, or thereafter becomes insane, or of unsound mind, and the accommodations in said almshouse are not adequate and proper, in the opinion of the said Secretary of the State Board of Charities, for his treatment and care, the said Secretary may cause his removal to the appropriate State Asylum for the Insane and he shall be received by the officer in charge of such asylum and maintained therein until duly discharged.

OHIO.

If any person in prison shall, after the commission of an offence, and before conviction, become insane * * * an examining court may be called in the manner provided in the Act entitled * * * and if such court shall find that such person became insane after the commission of the crime or misdemeanor of which he stands or charged indicted, and is still insane, the said court shall proceed and the prisoner shall for the time being, and until restored to reason be dealt with in like manner as other lunatics are required to be after inquest had, *provided*, however, that if said lunatic be discharged, the bond given for his support and safe-keeping shall also be conditioned that said lunatic shall when restored to reason answer to said crime or misdemeanor and abide the order of the court in the premises; and any such lunatic may, when restored to reason, be prosecuted for any offence committed by him previous to such insanity.

If any person, after being convicted of any crime or misdemeanor, and before the execution in whole or in part of the sentence of the court, become insane, it shall be the duty of the Governor of the State to inquire into the facts, and he may pardon such lunatic, and commute or suspend for the time being the execution in such manner, and for such a period as he may think proper, and may by his warrant to the Sheriff of the proper county, or Warden of the Ohio Penitentiary, order such lunatic to be conveyed to the asylum and there kept until restored to his reason. If the sentence of any such lunatic is suspended by the Governor, the sentence of the court shall be executed upon him after such period of suspension hath expired, unless otherwise directed by the Governor.

RHODE ISLAND.

If upon examination a judge is satisfied that the person thus imprisoned is insane or idiotic, he shall have the power to order the removal of such prisoner from the State prison or jail aforesaid, to be detained in the State Asylum for the Insane, if he can be there received, or if not in the Butler Hospital.

Such order of removal shall be for and during the term of said prisoner's sentence, and be directed to the Sheriff of the county in which such prisoner stands committed.

Any person removed as aforesaid, upon restoration to reason may, by an order of either of the judges of the Supreme Court in his discretion be remanded to the place of his original confinement, to serve out the remainder of his term of service.

MASSACHUSETTS.

The physician of the State Prison, as chairman with the Superintendents of the State Lunatic Hospital, shall constitute a commission for the examination of convicts in said prison alleged to be insane. Each commissioner shall receive for his services in such capacity his travelling expenses and three dollars a day for each day he is so employed.

The Commission shall investigate the case, and if in the opinion of the majority of them, the convict has become insane and his removal would be expedient, they shall so report, with their reasons, to a judge of the Superior Court, who shall forthwith issue his warrant under the seal of that court, directed to the Warden, authorizing him to remove the convict to one of the State lunatic hospitals, there to be kept till in the opinion of the Superintendent and Trustees thereof, he may be recommitted consistently with his health.

When a convict in the prison appears to be insane, the Warden or Inspector shall give notice to the chairman of said commission, who shall forthwith notify the members thereof to meet at the prison.

NEW HAMPSHIRE.

The Governor, with the advice of the Council, may remove to the Asylum, to be there kept at the expense of the State, any person confined in the State prison who is insane.

SOUTH CAROLINA.

Any judge of the circuit court is authorized to send to the lunatic asylum every person charged with the commission of any criminal offence who shall upon the trial before him prove to be *non compos mentis*, and the said judge is authorized to make all necessary orders to carry into effect this power.

TENNESSEE.

That section 5488 of the code of Tennessee be so amended as to read, whenever the physician reports to the keeper of the penitentiary that any convict is insane, and ought on that account to be removed to the lunatic asylum, the keeper shall cause such insane convict to be removed accordingly, there to remain until discharged by the physician of said lunatic asylum.

TEXAS AND IOWA.

If any person charged with, or convicted of any criminal offence be found to be insane in the court before which he is so charged or convicted, said court shall order him to be conveyed to and retained in the State Lunatic Asylum, and he shall be received and retained, until removed by the order of the court by which he was committed to the asylum.

If any person after being convicted of any crime or misdemeanor, and before the execution in whole or part of the sentence of the court, becomes insane, it shall be the duty of the Governor of the State to inquire into the facts, and he may pardon such lunatic or commute or suspend for the time being the execution, in such manner and for such a period, as he may think proper, and may by his warrant to the Sheriff of the proper county, or Warden of the Iowa penitentiary, order such lunatic to be conveyed to the hospital and there kept until restored to reason.

As before said, the State of New York has made provision for the care in hospitals of all her insane poor. For this she is to be commended; in this to be imitated. But the hospital or asylum referred to in the foregoing statutes, as that to which "insane convicts" and others are to be sent, is a lunatic asylum established by a statute of 1858,

ON THE PRISON GROUNDS

at Auburn, expressly for this object. In this, her *purpose* is most laudable; but the propriety of her *course* is most questionable, as will more fully appear in the sequel.

This Board had the honor, last year, of causing to be prepared and laid before the Senate, the draught of a bill "to provide for the care and keeping of the criminal insane of this commonwealth,—including those who may be acquitted of crime on the ground of insanity." And the proposition was, in general terms, that a department, a wing or a distinct building surrounded by a wall, of the hospital now under construction at Danville, should be so planned, arranged, completed and organized as to make it fit, suitable and convenient for the care, keeping and treatment of the classes of insane persons referred to. It may be proper to say that the Board had

CHIEFLY IN VIEW, THE MORE NUMEROUS CLASS;

those who were in prisons with criminals, without ever having been convicted of crime; and that they made their recommendation, so far as regards the less numerous class, the strictly "convict insane," on the assumption, which we have shown may fairly be made, that the vast majority of such convicts were really insane, or, at least, in the incipient or latent stages of insanity, at the time the acts charged against them as crimes, were committed.* They were cases of this sort, or this was the aspect of the cases we had in mind, and for which we sought relief; the others, the ten per cent. or so, we regarded as simply exceptions, which, at all events, should not vitiate the rule. We proposed but did not urge the bill; and, through misunderstanding, and in consequence of opposition from interested parties, it was lost.

At the late meeting in Baltimore of the Association of Medical Superintendents of Hospitals for the Insane, it was openly stated by a member from Pennsylvania that "that measure was defeated (I suppose) by the efforts of certain members of this association," and the statement was not contradicted. (See Journal of Insanity, Oct. 1873, page 236.)

This meeting of medical superintendents was a notable one.

---

* Report in relation to the insane convicts in the Eastern Penitentiary on February 24, 1873, by EDWARD TOWNSEND, Warden—number this date, 12.
W. W.   Confirmed lunatic on admission.
M. L.   Imbecile in mind on admission.
T. R.   Unsound mind on admission.
A. N.   Unsound mind on admission.
I. B. H. Imbecile on admission.
G. V.   Decidedly imbecile when admitted.
M. V. B. S. Very weak-minded on admission, since insane.
Dora S. Insane on admission and remains so.
Mary S. Insane on admission and had been an inmate of an insane asylum.
M McG. Very feeble-minded on admission.
E L.   Weak-minded, bordering on lunacy, when admitted.
P. L.   Insane on admission.

Report of EDWARD S. WRIGHT, Warden of Western Penitentiary, on the same subject, made at the same time. Number of insane convicts in Penitentiary, 8.
Prisoner No. 3324, mental health, impaired on admission.
"   "   3720,   "   "   "
"   "   3750,   "   "   "
"   "   3958,   "   "   "
"   "   4006,   "   "   "
"   "   4008,   "   "   "
"   "   4019,   "   insane on admission.
"   "   4030,   "   insane on admission.

Believing that the case of the proposed law just referred to, had not been fully understood, and wishing to have the subject freely and thoroughly ventilated, we addressed to the President of this association, the following communication:

Philadelphia, May 28th, 1873.

"DR. J. S. BUTLER,

"*President of Convention of Medical Superintendents for the Insane.*

"Dear sir,—The morning papers inform me that the important humanitarian body over which you preside, has assembled for the consideration of the interests of the insane in convention at Baltimore. On other like occasions, the commissioners of this board have been honored with an invitation,—to be represented, of course, in presence merely; but still we are glad to be apprised of your meeting by public announcement, and venture to address you on a subject of great interest to this Board, and one which, we think, has escaped any authoritative action of your body.

"We refer to the subject of the care of the 'criminal insane.' We are led to refer this matter to you *for action*, because of an unsuccessful effort made by this Board to have a precedent established by the Legislature of the State of Pennsylvania, to construct a department for this class *upon the grounds of the Hospital for the Insane at Danville, Penn'a.,* for the reception and treatment of (for the most part) the irresponsible insane, who are now incarcerated in the penitentiaries and jails of this Commonwealth.

"It is true that we did not press this matter upon the Legislature, believing that the simple proposition should be sufficient for favorable action; but as the higher advice of representatives from this State in your Convention prevailed to defeat the measure which we proposed, we feel justified in asking you to take such definite action as will have like influence in protecting the class, who are committed, in this State, at least, (I am glad to say not in all other States) to the miseries of a felon's doom.

"In noticing this subject I beg your permission to venture

on a few observations on the subject, and in doing so I express the mind of every member of this Board.

"It is a fact patent to all of us, that multitudes of irresponsible criminal insane are now in the prisons of many of the States, and it is equally true that the influence of the body known as the Association of Medical Superintendents of American Institutions for the Insane, has exercised a most potent and salutary influence, in shaping the legislation of the several States, in behalf of this afflicted class of their citizens.

"Believing that your influence will avail to check the enormous wrong which the class we refer to suffer, we ask your intervention in their behalf, and urge you to set forth a distinct and definite policy which shall satisfy its demands.

"We know that in Great Britain there are two asylums for the specially criminal insane; one at Broadmoor, not far from London, a distinct institution with accommodations for from five to six hundred inmates; and one at Perth, Scotland, under penal jurisdisdiction, but in charge of a special superintendent.

"We know that on the continent of Europe there is no special provision for the criminal insane; it being held by the most distinguished alienist physicians and so proclaimed in many works on psychological subjects, that insanity should level all distinctions; and, as Dr. Manning reports, that 'the great gulf which separates the convict from the honest man is bridged over by insanity; that when sick in body, the prisoner should be kept within his prison and treated for his malady, but when sick in mind, the prison should be opened and the badge of the convict be forgotten."

"In this view, the well known humanitarian, Miss Dix, concurred.

"We also know that in these United States there is an asylum for insane convicts at Auburn, New York, intended originally for the reception of such as became insane when convicts, but more recently for those, also, who have been acquitted on the ground of insanity. We know of no other special provision made for this class, unless it be in jails. In the State of Pennsylvania there are not, we think, over ten per cent. of the number who are now confined in the penitentiaries and jails, who, on the report of the wardens and prison-keepers, were not insane when sentenced, and of this small percentage, some, of course, were mentally imbecile or, in the incipient stage of insanity, when the crime was committed. The law holds them to be 'irresponsible,' and, still, they are held as felons by the act of the law. As has been well said 'the courts fail to detect the disability for want of a proper defence or because the mental disease is still latent.' The jails thus receive these forlorn 'wards of the State' forsaken by man, not, we believe, by God. We could enumerate instances of marked cruelty in individual cases, but we point only to the injustice which must inevitably oppress them, when subjected to the treatment of prisoners in the State and county jails: Their lightest affliction being perpetual incarceration within the limits of a cell, without the slightest consideration of their sufferings or their needs. This is the case, certainly, in Pennsylvania.

"There will be no dispute as to the impolicy as well as the wrong-doing of such 'proceedings.' These 'irresponsible' citizens are, as is often said, 'wards of the State.' Surely no official of the State, no private citizen, who is the head of a family, would overlook the claims of his own children. They would extend the solace and the help all the more for their infirmities.

"In the year 1871 the Massachusetts Board of Public Charities addressed communications to the Superintendents of the lunatic hospitals of that State, requesting their views on certain points. That which concerns this Board is the inquiry as to the *provision* which should be made for the class to whom we refer. It is highly honorable, in our judgment, to the intelligence as well as to the humanity of each of these distinguished gentlemen, that neither recommended that a hospital for the 'criminal insane' should be an appendage or an appurtenance of a prison, or built at all on prison grounds.

On the contrary, although one of them, to relieve the urgency of the case, admits that he has recommended the fitting up of a lunatic ward in the State Prison, to be placed under the special care of the prison physician, still he declares, 'there would be but little objection, aside from sentiment, to the treatment of lunatic convicts in a properly constructed hospital for the insane, where they would not mingle indiscriminately with the other classes of patients.' Another says, 'I would not advocate making it an adjunct of the State Prison, or any penal institution.' The last, after recommending that a distinct institution be established for the reception of this class, says, with the knowledge that they are provided for, [in Mass.] in the State lunatic hospitals, 'if the Superintendent and Trustees of any State lunatic hospital, and the general agent of the Board of State Charities, concur in the opinion that a patient of said hospital ought to be removed to said building, he should be so removed. This is the alternative to care and treatment in a general hospital for the insane: in Pennsylvania, [it would be] from a prison to a hospital.

"As the result of the investigations of this intelligent Commission, and the views forcibly presented by the eminent alienist physicians of their own State, viz., Drs. Godding, Earle, and Bemis, this cautious Board has recommended in their present report, just issued, *the establishment of a hospital for the 'criminal insane,' to be placed near enough one of the other State hospitals for the insane to be under the same administration.*

"This Board concurs in the principle which underlies this recommendation, as well as in its practical wisdom; for, as to the latter, it cannot be expected that any one State will incur the expense of an independent establishment for this class and the cost of its proper oversight and maintenance. As has been already stated, there is but one in England whose population approximates to our own, [that of the United States.] As to the former, there is no *moral ground* upon which the separation of the two classes can be based. It is simply the ground of disagreeableness, to those who conduct the institution, to a small proportion of the patients, and to some of their friends. It is 'sentiment;' and this we admit should be religiously regarded in the consideration of every provision for the insane. Let it not be overlooked in behalf of the class we are now considering! We say sentiment only, for the scheme proposed to our Legislature provided for a separate and secure building, separately enclosed with suitable walls, *but to be under the supervision of the Superintendent of the General Hospital*, on the same premises."

"Believing that our views have been clearly conveyed in this communication, and excusing its crudeness, by the obvious necessity of haste, I beg most respectfully to commit the subject to your thoughtful determination and action; and I trust that they may be so enlightened, as to reflect honor upon your body and yourselves individualy—not merely for the present, but for all time.

"I am most respectfully yours,

"GEO. L. HARRISON,
" *President.*"

When the association entered upon the consideration of this letter, the following resolutions were offered:

" WHEREAS, The proper disposal of that class of the insane, whose criminal acts require their seclusion and confinement, is a matter on which this association is requested to express an opinion,

" 1. *Resolved*, Therefore, as the opinion of this association, that neither jails and penitentiaries, nor ordinary hospitals for the insane are proper receptacles for this class of persons; but that they should be cared for in establishments designed expressly and solely for them.

" 2. *Resolved*, That under no circunstances should 'insane convicts' be associated with other insane persons, believing that such an association is not calculated to improve the condition of the latter, and that the best interests of the former require a special management, and architectural arrangements of a peculiar kind, both very different from such as are adapted to the needs of other classes of the insane.

"3. *Resolved*, also, that the example of the State of New York, which has thus provided for its 'criminal insane,' as they are usually called, be commended to imitation by other States, either singly or collectively."

We take the liberty of reproducing here some of the most note-worthy utterances which this discussion called forth in the association, as they are published in the journal of insanity, before cited.

Dr. Shew, Superintendent of the General Hospital for the Insane, Middletown, Conn., "If the resolutions refer to persons who commit acts which would be considered criminal were they not insane, I cannot concur in all the resolutions. Many of the patients received in our hospital commit those acts, and are sent to the hospital because they are dangerous to society;—dangerous as insane persons. It seems to me that there can be but one opinion, and that is that insane criminals should be separated entirely from patients in hospitals. First, because of the dangerous influence upon other patients; secondly, because of the odium which it brings on the institution, and the unpleasant feeling which the friends of the patients have in supposing or believing, that their loved-ones are associating daily and hourly with criminal persons."

"In practical experience I have not found that 'insane convicts' are particularly objectionable in themselves—not so much as Dr. Shurtleff and Dr. Curwen have." [Dr. Curwen has not given his remarks in the official publication.] "Three years ago the Legislature of Connecticut passed a law requiring the Trustees of the Hospital at Middletown to receive all insane convicts after a proper examination, which was specified, and a commission appointed. We had no separate provision, and were obliged to receive them in the hospital proper,

AND PLACE THEM IN ASSOCIATION

with the other patients. Since that time twelve insane convicts have been transferred from Wethersfield to Middletown; two of that number have escaped; one of them feigned insanity; arrangements had been made to transfer him to Wethersfield, but he escaped the very night before the transfer was to be made. Of the ten others, seven have been among the most valuable farm laborers, harmless, industrious and peaceable, and yet positively insane; much less dangerous than many of the chronic patients. One of the number has been very valuable the past few years, in sharpening the tools used by the stone-cutters in the erection of the two wings, saving the cost of one skilled mechanic. It was his trade and occupation, before being sent to prison.

NONE OF THE SEVEN WHO HAVE BEEN EMPLOYED EVER ATTEMPTED TO ESCAPE."

[*Why then was it, that in the case of the eight insane convicts sent to the Harrisburg Institution, five managed to escape?*]

"They are generally liked by the patients, and are not more troublesome than others. The friends of the patients ['paying' patients, doubtless] object to the association, and in my report last year, I called the attention of the Legislature to that fact, and asked that an appropriation be made for a separate building, distinct from the main hospital, a cottage simply, to provide for the insane convicts. * * * * During the present year, we hope to have a building for the *accommodation of twenty persons*, in which we will provide for all the insane convicts. There have been only three transferred from Wethersfield each year."

Dr. Shew, then, assuming that the population and resources of some of the States, and the number of their insane convicts, may be such as to warrant the construction in each, of an entirely separate hospital for their accommodation, with all the best appointments for their proper care and treatment,—proceeds to express, in that case, his preference for having such a hospital, intended exclusively for the insane convicts proper, erected on the grounds of the State Prison, rather than on those of a general hospital; but otherwise, and for other States, he clearly prefers such an arrangement as he has described at Middletown.

Dr. Compton of Mississippi:—

"The third resolution I think I would amend, because that condemns the action of my own State in this matter. It declares that under no circumstances should insane convicts be permitted to associate with other insane persons, believing that such association is not calculated to benefit the insane, &c. I would be very decidedly against the first part of the resolution, that, 'under no circumstances should they be associated.' *I would take them into my asylum, rather than let them remain in the penitentiary or jail. In the absence of the proper provisions, I would take them out of the penitentiary and jails, and put them into my asylum.*"

Dr. Earle, of Northampton, Mass.:

"I would put the convict insane in a separate institution, independent of all other institutions.

I WOULD PUT IN THE SAME PLACE,

those who have been tried for crime and acquitted on the ground of insanity; then those incendiary and homicidal patients, who never had been tried for crime. I would make the provision that they should be removed to that institution, but not unless it was decided by the Superintendent of the hospital, and the Board of State Charities and its agents; all these authorities must concur before a man who had committed a criminal act, and had not been convicted of crime, should be removed [not from the common hospital to the penitentiary or prison, but] from the common hospital to this institution. This applied only to the incendiary and homicidal class, because

OUR MOST DANGEROUS PATIENTS ARE NOT CONVICTS,

and have never been tried for crime and acquitted on the ground of insanity."

Dr. Gundry, of Athens, Ohio:

"In endorsing the action of the State of New York, we go further than my amendment would contemplate, because we endorse this course. They have done very well in providing a hospital for insane convicts, but with those insane convicts they send persons who are compelled to mingle with them, whose acts of violence were committed in their diseased condition. It is urged that this is a matter of expediency, because the hospitals are not able to contain them for various reasons.

IF THE HOSPITALS ARE NOT PROPERLY CONSTRUCTED MAKE THEM SO.

"If special arrangement are required for violent patients, have those special arrangements made." The doctor then goes on to speak with more kindness than respect, of Boards of State Charities, but with this we have nothing to do.

Dr. Smith, of Fulton, Missouri:—

"I must also object to that part of one of the resolutions, which endorses the New York law. Those conversant with this law inform us that one of its provisions requires that all acquitted on the ground of insanity, shall, in the discretion of the judge, be sent to the same institution designed for convicts." [And, he might have added, standing as a department of the State Prison.] "Such a provision as this I cannot endorse. * * * *Endorsing this law would be equivalent to endorsing the punishment of the insane, because of the acquittal of crime;* the penalty of assigning them to a position most repulsive to their feelings and those of their friends, and one that would not only retard but often prevent recovery". [What would the Doctor have said of sending them, *as we do*, not to a common hospital, but to a common prison?] "*We have patients in our institution, who, prior to admission, committed terrible deeds, and, no doubt, there are such in most hospitals for the insane.* We have fathers who killed their wives and children; and a mother who killed her husband, all under the influence of delusions in regard to different members of their families. These patients have been as orderly, quiet and pleasant as any in our building; have shown no tendency to violence, and exerted no injurious influence over others."

The resolutions were amended and finally passed as follows; and were transmitted to us as the response of the Association.

"WHEREAS, The President of the Board of Charities of Pennsylvania has requested that this Association should express its opinion in regard to the proper disposition of insane convicts, therefore,

"*Resolved*, 1. That neither the cells of penitentiaries and jails, nor the wards of ordinary hospitals for the insane are proper places for the custody and treatment of this class of the insane.

"2. That when the number of this class in any State (or in any two or more adjoining States which will unite in the project) is sufficient to justify such a course, these cases should be placed in a hospital specially provided for the purpose: and that until this can be done, they should be treated in a hospital connected with some prison, and not in the wards nor in separate buildings, upon any part of the grounds of an ordinary hospital for the insane."

The published report of the debate, from which we have made the foregoing citations, as containing important medical opinions bearing on the subject in hand, would have been more complete and fair, as well as less liable to misunderstanding, if the letter from this Board, which called it forth, had not been suppressed. It would then have appeared that both the debate and the final action of the Association failed to grasp the precise points presented in the letter. They treated the subject with reference to an ideal standard, rather than with reference to the actual laws and practice of Pennsylvania in the case.

The whole debate and the final action were eventually narrowed down to the case of "insane convicts" exclusively, instead of taking into view all the classes of the "criminal insane," so called, which were presented for their consideration.

It is instructive, however, to compare the resolutions finally adopted with those originally proposed.

1. Both sets of resolutions agree,—and so did, apparently every member of the Association, in the most emphatic manner—in the fundamental principle, that neither the cells of jails and penitentiaries, nor the wards of ordinary hospitals for the insane, are *proper receptacles for the custody and treatment* of that class of the insane, whose case was under consideration.

2. The resolutions adopted confine themselves to the care of

INSANE CONVICTS AS SUCH,

a portion only of the cases submitted for consideration, while the original preamble included the "proper disposal of that class of the insane, whose criminal acts require their seclusion and confinement." Precisely what class was intended to be thus described, might be doubted, but if simply "insane convicts" were intended, it was a very circuitous way of saying so.

3. It is not expressly and positively declared, in these, as in the former resolutions, that, under no circumstances, should "insane convicts" be associated with other insane persons; but merely that they should be treated

"IN A HOSPITAL SPECIALLY PROVIDED FOR THE PURPOSE."

It is left an open question whether or not other special classes of insane persons may be treated in the same specially provided hospital, *i. e.* supposing such hospital not to be on prison grounds, and at the same time not a department of any ordinary hospital for the insane.

4. The commendation of the New York plan, of sending other insane persons besides convicts to a hospital connected with a State prison, is carefully avoided.

5. A separate hospital for this class,—separate from prisons as well as ordinary hospitals,—is proposed as the proper and desirable plan—provided it can be had.

6. Until such a hospital can be had, it is proposed, as an imperfect, temporary and unsatisfactory substitute,—but as much better than giving "insane convicts" no special or remedial treatment at all, that they, *i. e.*

THE STRICTLY "INSANE CONVICTS" AS SUCH AND BY THEMSELVES,

should be treated in a hospital connected with some prison, rather than on the grounds of any "ordinary" hospital for the insane.

The conclusions thus reached, as far as they go, would be quite in harmony with the views of this Board, except, perhaps, in the last-mentioned particular; and, on that point, there might be no substantial disagreement, when the case is narrowed down to the precise circumstances contemplated, and the precise expressions employed. *It is, in terms, an undesirable alternative, which is thus presented.* We think, and we shall hope to show that it is

NEITHER REASONABLE NOR NECESSARY TO RESORT TO SUCH AN ALTERNATIVE AT ALL.

The plan of two or more States joining in the erection or support of a hospital for insane convicts is not new. Such a plan was proposed and drawn out at large by Dr. Edward Jarvis of Massachusetts, in 1857, in a very able and suggestive paper on the "criminal insane." We cannot but regard all such propositions as simply futile.

NO TWO OR MORE STATES WILL EVER COMBINE

in building a common hospital for their "insane convicts;" nor will any one State ever provide such a hospital for the use of other States. In reference to such joint action, the case of insane convicts is very different from that of the blind or deaf mutes or the ordinary insane. We may therefore dismiss such suggestions as visionary and illusory: And the fact that *United States* convicts are received into the convict prisons of several of the States, in the absence of a national prison, furnishes no parallel at all to the expedient suggested, of one State taking charge of another State's convicts. It may be quite possible, and fair, also, for a child to accommodate a parent in an emergency; and impracticable and unreasonable to extend like assistance to a fellow child. But let it be observed in any case, that we make no *objection* to the joint action of several States in the premises; we only express a decided opinion that it will never be brought about.

It remains, then, for each State, to make provision for herself. We must consider the subject in this point of view, if we are to give it any *practical* consideration at all. Now no one State,—not even New York or Pennsylvania, has such a number of *insane convicts*, in the strict sense of the terms, as would warrant the erection and equipment of a completely separate hospital for their exclusive care and treatment: Such a hospital as should furnish them the best supervision and attendance—and nothing less ought to be furnished them. The number of such convicts in this State is probably not many more at any one time, than could be accommodated in Dr. Shew's "little cottage" attached to his hospital. For it is to be observed that the magnitude of the existing evil in this particular case, consists not so much in its numerical extent, as

IN THE PRINCIPLE INVOLVED, AND IN ITS RAMIFYING CONNECTIONS.

The State has no right to offset economy against an injustice or against inhumanity; but she has a right, in doing justice, to study economy; and she is likely more fully to meet the demands of justice and humanity on the whole and in the long run, when she makes her plans with a far-seeing and systematic economy, than when she indulges in spasmodic extravagance.

It may be assumed as another settled thing, that

THE STATE WILL NEVER ESTABLISH AN ENTIRELY SEPARATE HOSPITAL,

separate from all connection either with prisons or with ordinary hospitals,

FOR THE EXCLUSIVE ACCOMMODATION OF TWENTY OR THIRTY "INSANE CONVICTS;"

and provide it with all the appointments of a complete hospital for the care and treatment of the insane. This plan may be dismissed as equally visionary and illusory with the other.

But it is not to be forgotten that, besides the strictly insane convicts, there are other analogous and closely bordering classes of insane persons yet to be provided for in this State: (1) Those who have been convicted of crime, but have served out their sentences and continue insane; and of these, there may be nearly as many as of the others. (2) Those who have been charged with crime, but are found insane before trial or sentence;—these are a class nearly as numerous, probably, as the insane convicts, and yet they are not insane convicts. (3) Those who have committed terrible acts of violence or destruction, as homicide, arson, burglary &c., and have been acquitted of crime on the ground of insanity; but, who, for the safety of the community, must be kept under the most watchful and perhaps rigorous restraint, as well as provided with the most skillful curative treatment.

ALL THESE CLASSES ARE NOW IN OUR JAILS AND PENITENTIARIES OR POORHOUSES,

or are by law liable to be there, and other classes beside them;* and their case is to be provided for as well as that

---

*The following facts are reported by the General Agent of this Board, under date: Nov. 1 Insane frequently sent into prison, sometimes as many as eight or ten at a time, who are kept until the court decides what disposition to make of them.
One lunatic sentenced Nov. 13th, 1868, for ten days, to enter bail for good behavior. In

of the strictly insane convicts. And even if a special hospital should be provided for insane convicts, in connection with some prison or penitentiary and on the prison ground, rather than in connection with one of the State Lunatic Asylums, and with the imperfect appointments and supervision which must needs characterize such an establishment, considered as a mere department of the prison; we will not ask now whether this is all that is due to the "insane convicts" themselves, but we do ask whether those other classes of insane persons ought to be

SENT TO SUCH A HOSPITAL, TO ASSOCIATE WITH THE INSANE CONVICTS IN A DEPARTMENT OF A PRISON?

Either that, or left in the cells of the jails and penitentiaries, or poorhouses, *where they are*. But it is asked, why not send them, in such a case, to the ordinary lunatic hospitals? We answer by asking why they are *not* uniformly sent there now? or, why, when sent there, they are exposed to be remanded to the prison cells?

It may be said that this very class of "criminal insane" *are* in the hospitals, and that the "returns" to this Board from these institutions present this fact continually. We have not denied or disputed the fact. We have not found fault with the little good that is done; but only with the great wrong-doing which so completely obscures and overshadows it. The law should declare the rights of every citizen, and vindicate them uniformly and without exception, especially the rights of the poor and defenceless.

In fact the whole question is narrowed down to these points:

---

default of bail he has been confined ever since. The cause of his detention is the want of suitable accommodations in the County Almshouse.

Eight insane were sent to this prison in 1872, all of whom were transferred to the County Almshouse.

One lunatic confined since last winter, was sent here from the poorhouse for safety, not being able to keep her at the latter.

One "criminal insane" confined nearly six years under a "charge" of arson.

One man charged with having stolen a horse, was acquitted on the ground of ground of insanity, but is still confined.

One committed for threat to kill.

One man not charged with crime, committed for safe-keeping.

Insane frequently committed.

One charged with attempt to shoot, suffers under mental disorder.

Insane frequently committed.

1. It is agreed on all hands that neither prisons nor ordinary hospitals, with the ordinary arrangements, are fit places for the custody and treatment of "insane convicts."

2. The co-operation of several States in establishing or maintaining a special hospital for that purpose, is out of the question.

3. It is equally out of the question for one State, for this State, to provide for the exclusive use of this class of insane, an entirely separate institution, with the proper hospital equipment and superintendence.

4. Their special hospital, therefore, if they are to have any, must either be upon the grounds of a prison and an appendage to it, with the imperfect and insufficient supervision of the prison physician, the attendance of prison overseers or keepers, and the atmosphere of prison associations, or

UPON THE GROUNDS OF SOME STATE HOSPITAL,

so as to be under the same supervision of high and appropriate medical character, the same attendance and the same curative influences; though, while a department of the hospital, it may be made as completely secure and kept as separate from it as may be thought best,—to be denominated not "the convict department" or "the criminal department," but simply "the special department of such a hospital." This remains

THE ONLY PRACTICAL ALTERNATIVE.

If the former course is chosen, the patients will not be secured *that degree of skillful treatment and of humane and careful attendance*, which is their due, and without which there is small prospect of their recovery; and, what is perhaps more, it would be

UTTERLY UNJUST AND OUTRAGEOUS TO RETAIN THOSE OTHER CLASSES OF THE INSANE,—

if placed in the same hospital with the convicts,—not only in connection with those convicts, but in association with the scenes and the character and the odium of the penitentiary. Even that might, indeed, be an improvement upon their present condition; but in principle and in fact the wrong inflicted upon them would be the same; they would still be

CONSIGNED TO THE PENITENTIARY.

Either this, we say again, or they must be sent to ordinary hospitals.

If, on the other hand, the latter alternative is chosen, then *this special or separate department of the hospital, instead of being regarded as properly intended for insane convicts, may and should be regarded as intended chiefly and in the first instance, for the accommodation and safe-keeping of the three, and perhaps other, classes of insane persons above described; and the far less numerous class of insane convicts may be regarded as being admitted, in the character of insane, to a higher position than, as convicts, they could claim;* and, meantime, the infamy of incarcerating innocent and helpless men and women in the criminal's dungeon would be done away, while the ordinary hospitals would be relieved from the charge of some of the insane, who require the most special and expensive arrangements for their safe-keeping. *It would not be that the insane of these other classes would be thrust into a convict hospital; but convicts would be admitted to a hospital intended for other classes.* And even this need not continue, *and should continue no longer than till the State should feel justified in establishing a totally separate hospital for the insane convicts themselves.* If, till then, it be thought a wrong to these other classes of lunatics, that convicts, though insane, like themselves and equally irresponsible, should be thrust upon their society at all, we answer that among these classes as little of actual association or intercourse might be allowed, even within this separate department or wing of the hospital, which they would occupy in common, as might be thought advisable. At all events, to be obliged to be associated with insane convicts in a common hospital is *small ground for complaint,* in comparison to being thrust into association with felons, sane as well as insane, in a common prison. As to the inmates of the other departments of the general hospital, on whose grounds this special and separate department would stand, for us or for their friends to think of any hardship or degradation to them in consequence of their *separate connection with this department,* is, surely, nothing less than the most superlative extravagance of sentimental fastidiousness; especially when it is remembered that the whole hospital is furnished by the liberality of the State for the

ACCOMMODATION OF POOR AND DESTITUTE INSANE PEOPLE;

people, too, who would, otherwise, be miserably and hopelessly languishing in poorhouses and prisons.

And, besides, the objection to making the provision we have suggested for the criminal insane, so called, in a separate department on hospital grounds, leaves only the alternative of keeping them in *direct association* with unoffending insane in the poorhouses, where they are constantly sent; so that, as these are not "paying" patients, it would seem that they are to be left out in a discussion of the subject, and their rights are not to be considered. Let us not continue, as a State, to inflict, by the wholesale, upon our helpless fellow creatures the most outrageous wrongs, until we can be sure of doing right with the most mathematical precision, or

AFTER THE NICEST AND MOST PERFECT IDEAL AND SENTIMENTAL MODEL.

Let us not strain out the gnat, while we unhesitatingly swallow the camel!

The suggestion, that in dealing with insane convicts, one of two things must occur, namely, that, "you must make a prison of the hospital or a hospital of the prison"—and that the latter alternative is wiser and more humane, is, we consider, more specious than sound. We think, we have shown that the tendency of the prevailing system in this State is to "imprison" numbers of irresponsible insane, whose clear right it is to enjoy "hospital" care. Surely this should be reversed even, if need be, at the inconvenience, (if it be such) to the hospital of caring for a few individuals who have been guilty of crime, and have since become insane.

One of the strangest and most inhuman suggestions in regard to the insanity of convicts, is, that it should be considered as "a part of their punishment." So far as their whole punishment is to be regarded as a divine infliction, the suggestion is entirely true, and God's ways can undoubtedly be vindicated; but, from this point of view, the same is true of *all cases* of insanity: they are all visitations of Divine Providence, and, as such, are just and not to be murmured against. However great the suffering, it is, in every case, a righteous infliction. But to say that insanity is any part of the punishment inflicted on convicts by the sentence of human law, is simply false. If it were true; if, by the sentence of the law, men were to be driven insane, as a punishment for their crimes,—some, and not others; without any "rhyme or reason" in making the distinction,—it would be nothing short of the grossest and most detestable inhumanity as well as injustice. In the case of convicts, insanity is no more a part of their punishment, than any other disease. If a convict is seized with fever or small-pox, shall we say "it is a part of his punishment," and so leave him to its consequences? No, we are to give him such diet and care and medical treatment as will be likely *to ensure his recovery in the shortest time.* This can be done in the prison hospital. All we ask, is, that the same be done in case the disease is insanity. If this can be done,—if *the best* medical superintendence and care can be provided in connection with the prison, let it be done; we have no objection to make. But if not, if better provision can be supplied for these purposes, in connection with some established hospital, and at vastly less cost, then let this latter course be preferred and adopted.

The whole matter is narrowed to a question of expediency

and expense. If the State is prepared to meet the expense of providing the appointments of a first-class hospital, expressly and exclusively for twenty or thirty "insane convicts;" very well, let them be forthwith provided. But, if not, let some other *adequate* provision be made. At all events, *let not helpless lunatics be left incarcerated in the cells of prisons and poorhouses.*

We have said before, and we now say again, that neither insanity nor the privation of proper treatment in case of insanity, is any part of the sentence imposed upon convicts by law; and if there are still any who maintain that insanity is to be regarded as "a part of the convict's punishment," we beg only to add that such views as these are not shared in by the distinguished medical gentlemen, nor by the eminent philanthropic citizens, who have intelligently, and with full knowledge of the import of what they have done, set their hands to the accompanying

MEMORIALS

to the Legislature, praying your honorable bodies to redress the wrongs not merely or chiefly of insane convicts, but of the several classes of insane poor, upon whose defence we have entered, against not only the injurious insinuations of interested parties, but the actual personal injuries and sufferings, which are continuously heaped upon them, in defiance of every impulse of humanity, as well as every sober and righteous conviction of reason and judgment.

To the Board of Public Charities of the State of Pennsylvania.

The undersigned, practising physicians of the cities of Pittsburg and Allegheny, request your Board to take action looking to the repeal or modification of some of the provisions of law in relation to the treatment of the insane, more especially of those who have been acquitted on the ground of insanity, or who have become insane while incarcerated in prison or penitentiary.

We understand that the laws of this State in reference to these unfortunates are such, that in some cases, the courts are expressly forbidden to commit them to the hospitals unless they are deemed *speedily curable*; and that in cases where insane criminals or persons *acquitted* on the ground of insanity, have been sent by the court to the hospital, the Board of Managers and Superintendent or physician, if they deem them incurable, may send them back to the jail or penitentiary from which they came.

We are assured that such treatment of the insane, whether criminals or not, is inhuman; and knowing as we do that a prison or penitentiary is not, and cannot be a fitting place for the treatment of human beings so sadly afflicted, whether incurable or not, we earnestly appeal to you, and through you, to the Legislature of our State to have such a change made in the laws as will effectually prevent the exposure of the insane of any class, to incarceration in our prisons, jails, or penitentiaries.

Yours, &c.,

ANDREW FLEMING, M. D.
GEO. D. BRUCE, M. D.
H. T. COFFEY, M. D.
F. LE MOYNE, M. D.
W. J. ESTEP, M. D.
J. N. DICKSON, M. D.
THOS. W. SHAW, M. D.
JOHN DICKSON, M. D.
A. W. McCOY, M. D.
JOHN S. DICKSON, M. D.
W. SNIVELY, M. D.

A. M. POLLOCK, M. D.
W. C. REITER, M. D.
JULIAN ROGERS, M. D.
R. B. MOWRY, M. D.
C. B. KING, M. D.
J. B. MURDOCH, M. D.
W. R. HAMILTON, M. D.
JAS. KING, M. D.
JAS. McCANN, M. D.
T. C. RHOADS, M. D.
JAMES MACFARLANE, M. D.

Pittsburgh, December, 1873.

TO THE LEGISLATURE OF PENNSYLVANIA,
Philadelphia, December, 1873.

The undersigned, members of the Medical Profession, being aware of the sad condition of the "poor" and the "criminal" insane, who are suffering cruel personal wrongs and constant deterioration of their mental and bodily condition, in the jails and poorhouses of the State, respectfully appeal to your honorable bodies to provide such legislation, as will effectually secure the admission and detention of these classes in the State hospitals for the insane, so long as their malady requires it.

We believe that both humanity and public policy demand such legislation for the relief of wrongful suffering, and for the restoration to health and usefulness, of these afflicted and injured classes.

S. D. GROSS, M.D.
JOSEPH PANCOAST, M.D.
ALFRED STILLE, M.D.
FRANCIS G. SMITH, M.D.
S. WEIR MITCHELL, M.D.
WILLIAM PEPPER, M.D.
D. HAYES AGNEW, M.D.
J. FORSYTH MEIGS, M.D.
EDW. HARTSHORNE, M.D.
CASPAR MORRIS, M.D.
J. M. DACOSTA, M.D.
HIRAM CORSON, M.D.
HORATIO C. WOOD, M.D.
JOHN H. PACKARD, M.D.
F. F. MAURY, M.D.

TO THE SENATE AND HOUSE OF REPRESENTATIVES OF PENNSYLVANIA:

We gladly unite our names with those of the eminent jurists, the distinguished physicians, the inspectors and wardens of the penitentiaries, and other noted personages, familiar with the subject, in the appeal of the Board of Public Charities to your honorable bodies, to redress, by proper legislation, the wrongs of the "poor" and the "criminal" insane, who are now consigned to the jails and almshouses of the State; and who should, properly, be placed in the State Hospitals for the insane, which were established by the public for their reception, their care and remedial treatment.

JAMES J. BARCLAY,	WM. BACON STEVENS,
JOS. R. CHANDLER,	JNO. WELSH,
MAHLON H. DICKINSON,	CALEB COPE,
HENRY C. CAREY,	JOHN M. WHITALL,
ISAAC LEA,	WM. BIGLER,
JNO. O. JAMES,	ASA WHITNEY,
JAMES THOMPSON,	M. SIMPSON,
late Chief Justice.	*Bishop.*

DECEMBER 1, 1873.

After the fullest investigation of facts and the maturest reflection upon the case, we are constrained to declare that, in our clear conviction and judgment, every consideration of humanity, justice, propriety and expediency, is combined in favor of placing the special hospital for the "criminal insane," so called, *including incidentally and temporarily "insane convicts,"*

ON THE GROUNDS OF SOME STATE HOSPITAL,

so as to be under a common superintendence therewith, rather than within the purlieus of any prison.

We, therefore, most earnestly renew our recommendation that such a separate hospital department be speedily provided, with the proper construction and arrangements for the purposes indicated, on the grounds of the Danville Hospital.

We, further, feel constrained to suggest,—and we do it with much hesitation, and with sincere respect for all parties,—that, in forming a judgment on this scheme, a preponderating weight ought not to be attached to the opinions of parties, who may have any personal interest or convenience involved in the question, however respectable they may be, and even though they present themselves in the character of experts.

THE AUTHORITY OF EXPERTS IS LIMITED

to their particular professional sphere. Their proper office is to serve as *witnesses* and not as *judges*; and any intelligent and disinterested layman, who by personal observation, and thorough study, has made himself acquainted with the condition of the insane in our penitentiaries, jails, poorhouses and hospitals, is as well (perhaps better) qualified to judge, as they are, of the broad features of any plan proposed for ameliorating their condition—to judge what is consistent with or demanded by the dictates of justice, humanity and the public good.

We beg also to suggest, that for examining and determining what persons should be transferred from the prisons or poorhouses or other hospitals, to the separate hospital department above recommended, or therefrom to prison or the other hospitals, the law should provide that, either the Board of Public Charities by their general agent, or some other commissioner or commissioners specially appointed,—who should make themselves thoroughly acquainted with the condition and wants of the insane throughout the Commonwealth (i. e. of such as are kept under detention and restraint), who could be supposed to have no interests to subserve but those of justice, humanity and the public good, and who would act systematically and on general and impartial principles,—should

HAVE THE ULTIMATE CONTROL,

with such *advice* from the superintendents of the State hospitals and other experts as they may require; or as in the case of the New York law in this behalf, with the aid and advice of a commissioner of lunacy, specially appointed to aid the Board of Public Charities in their action.

If your honorable bodies should prefer the appointment of an independent commission, this Board will, of course, be entirely satisfied.

In all this, we presume, of course, that the courts would, in the first instance, make such disposition of the insane, who come under their judicial cognizance, as they should by law be authorized or required to do. Provision might also be made for carrying out any decision of the aforesaid commission or of the General Agent of this Board, which may be alleged to be erroneous or unjust, to some court to be reviewed and either confirmed or reversed. It is remarkable that in the late convention of Superintendents of the insane, to which reference has before been made, one of its members, having alluded to the provision of the New York law, empowering a judge to dispose, according to his discretion, of persons acquitted of murder and other crimes on the ground of insanity—sending them either to a convict hospital or some other, exclaimed, "Too great a sweep of power for one man!" And almost immediately after another member naively declared that "persons acquitted of a criminal act on the ground of insanity should be placed in the hospital for the insane, and the moment the superintendent considers him a fit subject for the asylum for convicts, he should be sent there!"

The truth is the very fact of the malady being obscure, and thus causing the general public to neglect its victims, excepting through mere curiosity, makes it important that the State, representing the community, should have a special agency whose duty it shall be to scrutinize the condition and needs of this class. Such a commission can understand these, as well as the physicians or attendants, and have no considerations of personal convenience to warp the judgment. The simple point of *diagnosis* of the particular phase of the malady is all in which he would necessarily be deficient.

It is the universal practice of governments which appoint such commissions, to constitute them of laymen.

We have said that the wrongs of the insane in prisons and poorhouses continue as they were, when Miss Dix's "Memorial" caused the State to provide a hospital for their alleviation.

We now say that, although every hospital built and projected, has been recommended to the Legislature with the same view, and, seemingly, with the same design, the system pursued has never extinguished and never will extinguish or even abate the evil. There are twelve hundred of these (outside of Philadelphia, where alone there are one thousand and fifty in the almshouse asylum,) suffering incarceration and neglect. The unnecessary costliness of these hospital establishments, for the indigent insane, and the liberal admission into them of "paying patients," forbid the realization of the intentions and the desires of the Legislature and the public.

In Conclusion,

we think we may assume the following as established principles or settled points

1. The State is bound to provide, not only for the safekeeping, but for the proper care and treatment of all her insane poor.

2. Neither jails, penitentiaries nor poorhouses are proper places for their detention or treatment, whatever may be the character of their insanity, or whether it be recent or of long standing—curable or incurable.

3. A person, while insane can be guilty of no crime, and it is both unjust and inhuman to consign innocent men and women to the ignominious cells of jails and penitentiaries, or to the foul kennels of poorhouses, simply because, though insane and irresponsible, they are "dangerous to be at large."

4. Even insane convicts ought not to be retained in the cells of prisons, but transferred to some hospital where they may be both safely kept and receive appropriate medical treatment.

In view of the foregoing admitted facts and principles, this Board begs to renew and repeat,

BY WAY OF SUMMARY, THE FOLLOWING RECOMMENDATIONS,

and most earnestly to urge them upon the attention of the Legislature.

1. That the State should make prompt and adequate provision in General State Hospitals *for all the insane poor* in the Commonwealth, determine by law how their expenses should be paid, require the several counties either to make equally suitable provision in proper hospitals for their insane poor, or to send them to the State Hospitals, and require the authorities of these hospitals to receive and retain them, as long as they need hospital care.

2. That a separate wing or department of one of the State Hospitals,—to be under the charge of its superintendent,—should be suitably constructed, arranged and equipped for the reception, custody and proper medical treatment (1) of those persons who continue insane after completing the period of their sentence for crime; (2) of those who, being charged with the commission of crime while sane, are adjudged insane before trial or sentence, (3) of those who are acquitted of certain crimes, as murder, arson, rape, burglary, &c., on the ground of insanity, and are adjudged too dangerous to be discharged, and, (4) perhaps, of other dangerous lunatics;—all these to be sent either to this department, or to the ordinary hospitals, according to the discretion of the court or of the proper commission.

3. That all other insane persons, who are brought up for the sentence of the courts, should be sent to the ordinary hospitals,

SO THAT NO INSANE PERSONS IN ANY CASE SHOULD BE COMMITTED TO PRISON.

4. That, *until an entirely separate hospital may be provided for their accommodation, "insane convicts" should be admitted to appropriate quarters in the above mentioned special department*,—their insanity to be ascertained and their transfer regulated according to provisions of law, and they themselves allowed as much or as little association with the other inmates of this department as the Superintendent of the hospital shall judge proper and expedient.

5. That a special Commission, appointed for the purpose,

or the Board of Public Charities of the Commonwealth, be authorized to transfer from the other State hospitals to the special department above proposed, and from that to the ordinary hospitals, such persons as upon due examination and inquiry, shall be judged proper. Whether this same Commission should have authority to remove insane persons from *prison* to the special hospital department, we leave without any expression of opinion. Definite provisions as to this might be prescribed by statute.

6. Inasmuch as there are strong and well founded objections to condemning any person as *incurably insane* beforehand, and as the presence of incurables is no more disadvantageous to the curable, and often less so, than some others who are curable, the Board are not prepared to recommend their systematic separation, but, under the presumption that

GENERAL HOSPITALS

will be provided for all the insane poor,—leave them to be retained in the several hospitals and distributed in each as the Superintendents may deem most advisable.

Such are our recommendations, and we present and urge them, not as theories, but as practical suggestions, looking to positive and immediate action.

We beg to call the particular attention of the members of the General Assembly to the fact that most of these recommendations are supported and guaranteed, not by the MERE OPINION, BUT BY THE DIRECT TESTIMONY OF THIS BOARD AND ITS GENERAL AGENT; and not only so, but by both the opinions and the testimony of the present and former JUDGES OF OUR CRIMINAL COURTS, the JUDGES OF THE SUPREME COURT, and by the INSPECTORS AND WARDENS OF OUR PENITENTIARIES, as well as by those of many Superintendents of the insane whose declarations, on this behalf, are embodied in this report: as also by those of LEARNED PHYSICIANS and INTELLIGENT PHILANTHROPISTS, who have made the facts of this case a subject of special examination and study;—to which many other names might have been added from all parts of the State, if pains had been taken to secure them:—and, finally, by the EXAMPLE AND EXPERIENCE OF OTHER STATES.

Respectfully submitted,

GEO. L. HARRISON,
President.

G. DAWSON COLEMAN,
HIESTER CLYMER,
WILLIAM BAKEWELL,
GEORGE BULLOCK,
A. C. NOYES,
FRANCIS WELLS,
DILLER LUTHER, M.D.
General Agent.

HARRISBURG, *December 31st,* 1873.

www.ingramcontent.com/pod-product-compliance
Lightning Source LLC
Chambersburg PA
CBHW031601170426
43196CB00032B/984